THE BIRDS THEY SANG

In memory of my godfather John Pomian and my aunt Elizabeth Łubieńska, who always encouraged me to pursue my interest in birds

Stanisław Łubieński

THE BIRDS
THEY SANG

Birds and People in Life and Art

The Westbourne Press

THE WESTBOURNE PRESS
26 Westbourne Grove, London W2 5RH
www.westbournepress.co.uk

Published in Great Britain 2020 by The Westbourne Press

First published in Polish as *Dwanaście srok za ogon*
in 2016 by Wydawnictwo Czarne

This book has been published with the support
of the ©POLAND Translation Program

Printed and bound by CPI Group (UK) Ltd, Croydon, CR0 4YY

Jacket design and illustrations by James Nunn

A full CIP record for this book is available from the British Library.

ISBN 978 1 908906 36 6
eISBN 978 1 908906 37 3

The FSC® label means that materials used for the
product have been responsibly sourced.

CONTENTS

INTRODUCTION

LET THIS BE MY LETTER of recommendation. I've been interested in birds since I started primary school, though I have to admit that my passion didn't arise of its own accord. Of course, I'd prefer to put it down to myself – to my intelligence, my curiosity, my originality. But my interest came through imitation. My guide into the world of ornithology was my cousin Michaś, two years older than me. I admired him and copied him. I sought his attention and followed him around.

Every year we'd take family vacations in the Masurian Lakes. We'd listen to the hooting of a Tengmalm's owl in a narrow inlet of Seksty Lake; from close up, we'd watch kingfishers fishing. We'd discuss whether a bird seen from the car could have been a short-toed eagle. In this way, I gradually immersed myself in the world of birds. I picked out my first binoculars from the cornucopia of Russian goods laid out on camp beds at the Banacha market. The Soviet lenses were pretty decent and besides, they were the only kind available.

Many ornithologists I know have some kind of founding myth about their own passion. Witek had a canary. He never liked it that much; the bird's noisy attention seeking got on his nerves. He'd grudgingly fill its water feeder. But who knows, if it wasn't for that darned canary Witek might have chosen an entirely different line of work. Kasia, from earliest childhood, used to stare at a stuffed grey gull that hung over her bed. As for me, I'd pinned two postcards over mine. One, which my father had brought back from Italy, bore a photograph of a young sparrow. The other was a copy of a drawing of a little owl by Dürer. Today I couldn't say with any certainty if those postcards had always been there, or if they appeared before or after the Soviet binoculars came along.

Or perhaps my journey with birds began with the word, not the image? My mother read to me a lot. Irena Jurgielewiczowa's *Four Feathered Friends* made a particular impression on me. It was the story of four young sparrows in Warsaw's Old Town: boastful Cresty, who was born under the roof of Writers House; quarrelsome Featherball; sickly Blackeye; and melancholy, withdrawn Saynought. Each bird had its own ambitions, its sympathies, and an entirely human character. I clearly remember the lump in my throat at the chapter titled 'Poor Little Grayling', in which one of the secondary characters is killed by a group of boys. I also recall trembling when Cresty was wounded and ended up in an old lady's apartment. How could I fail to identify with the sparrows of Warsaw after this?

At home we had only one bird book, Černy and Drchal's *Which Bird Is That?* I've no idea where it came from – no one in the family was interested in birds. My parents knew little about nature; the only animals we really liked are dogs. Nobody hunted. The sole trace of anything to do with hunting was a

A house sparrow

blackened alligator skin that hung in my uncle's house in Opole. It must have been 100 years old. I used to imagine it had been left to the family by the zoologist Konstanty Jelski, a distant relation, who had gone on expeditions to South America.

I wasn't fond of that first bird book of mine. I didn't like the drawings; the whole thing was on the gloomy side and, for as long as I can remember, the spine was cracked on page 130. I remember that was the page with the auks, the European penguins, seabirds that are poor flyers and that appear on the waters off Poland only in winter. They were something completely beyond the reach of a child in Warsaw. But. Even when I was looking for small songbirds, the book would always fall open at the auk page.

Which Bird Is That? was soon exiled. I took it to our weekend cottage and abandoned it there, prey to damp and mould. Its place was soon taken by Jan Sokołowski's *Birds of Poland*, which had large colour illustrations (though in places the colours had faded), and contained fascinating though often out-of-date information, such as a report that in 1913 a griffon vulture had nested in the Pieniny Mountains. The book was not very thick and its descriptions were terse, with a lot of white space on each page. These days bird books are packed solid with facts and guide books look like little bricks.

For a time I thought about buying a cockatiel, but I wasn't convinced about having a prisoner in the house. Pet shops sold only exotic birds – not the kind I could find in the neighbourhood, and those were the ones I wanted to get to know better. The creatures in cages weren't really birds at all, but rather posturing, wheedling imitations. I wanted a wild animal. Michaś found a young rook that we fed with farmer's cheese and which in vain we urged to fly. We'd throw it up in the air and it would caw resentfully, spread its wings, and drop gently onto the grass. Something was wrong with it. Its parents had probably figured out that their chick was not going to thrive and had thrown it out of the nest.

Bird guides are often referred to by the names of their authors. So then, I liked my Sokołowski. But the real breakthrough was *Birds of Europe*, edited by Kazimierz A. Dobrowolski, with plates by Władysław Siwek. The book was modern and up to date. Its layout recalled the American Peterson Guides, with clear and colourful illustrations. Alongside the descriptions of the various species were black-and-white drawings showing the bird's distinctive behaviours. I laboriously copied 'The common tern fishing' or 'The courtship flight of the common snipe'. Taking my cue from serious ornithologists, I began to keep a notebook with my sightings: '1 August: saw several mallards and coots in the park. 2 August: nothing but black-headed gulls today.'

At home I have an A4 composition book that my Grandmother Janka bought me. 'Stanisław Łubieński, BIRDS.' For some time around 1993, I pasted into it articles about animals that I came across (in some cases, judging by the round yellow stains, I must have used gum arabic instead of a school glue stick). My grandmother found cuttings for me in the *Kulisy* and *Przekrój* weeklies. They're professionally recorded – after all, grandmother was a librarian. For example, a piece about how at the height of the Polish summer many species begin their migration to Africa, captioned 'The Last Chicks'; underneath, in Grandmother's spidery handwriting: *Przekrój*, 8 August 1993.

I mainly cut out articles from *Gazeta Wyborcza*. Most are by Adam Wajrak. Some include a call for action: in the Omulew Valley in the former Ostrołęka Voivodeship people were hunting black grouse during the lekking season (lekking being the gathering of males to display in order to attract mates). Others are tourism-orientated: in the Bieszczady Mountains eagles can be seen circling above fast-food kiosks. Others still are educational: how to behave during a walk in the woods. For a year Krzysztof Filcek wrote about birds for the same newspaper. The series was called 'Taking your binoculars for a walk' and explained how and where to begin birding as a hobby. Engaging, matter-of-fact texts written by a true enthusiast.

At school my classmates found my interests amusing. Curiosity about birds provided good material for jokes (as it occasionally still does today, by the way). I can't say I suffered especially for that reason; there's always a price to pay for eccentricities. In biology I couldn't wait for us to get to zoology, but we barely touched on birds. The teacher knew little about the life of birds and couldn't even identify common species. I remember her helplessness when a classmate brought in some blue tit chicks found in the park. They probably came to a bad end, like the two gerbils in the back room of the biology lab. One morning we came in to find that they'd engaged in a fratricidal battle, as a result of which one of the gerbils lay dead with its leg bitten off, while the other was foraging calmly in the sawdust lining the cage.

I used to go looking for birds in our allotment garden or in the park, while we were playing football. I would stop and stare if I caught sight of some unfamiliar shape in the sky. I remember my parents' wonder when I spotted a woodpecker flying past in a report on the television news. 'Undulating flight,' I explained casually, though my identification would have required a little more clarification. To this day my brother remembers a note I made in my guide book of the sound made by one of the birds of prey: 'glee-eh glee-eh glee-eyon'. In 1994, my mother, Uncle Tomek, Michaś and I went to Hungary – my first foreign birding trip. It was organised by Maciej Zimowski, known later in Kraków literary circles as Maciej Kaczka, or Maciej the Duck.

In our forty-strong party there were seasoned middle-aged birders, a few young devotees and a handful of people who were not birdwatchers. I don't recall any conflicts or complaints: naturalists tend to be impervious to discomfort. Besides, the natural world offers its compensations. On a branch over our tent, we'd already seen the nest of a lesser grey shrike, while right outside the gate there were red-footed falcons, small birds of prey that feed mostly on insects. In the night, it turned out that the campground was guarded by three species of owl. There was a beautiful white lady – the barn owl – and a family of little owls whose chick almost fell on our heads when it was attempting awkwardly to perch on a gutter. Last, there was a squat tawny owl, the most secretive of the group, which would sit alone on the picket fence at the edge of the camp.

My impressions from my summer vacation were a bit different from those of my classmates. I didn't remember the cities, monuments or shops of Hungary; only the image of the sun-scorched steppe, the infernal heat, and the sunburned faces of my travelling companions. A walk on the cracked-earth bed of a dried-up lake, and a spoon-shaped beak submerged in the mud – of its former owner, a spoonbill, nothing else remained. And also my mother's coy *bon mot* at the ice-breaking party: 'I'm old enough to have seen a dodo.'

I still have a mental slide show of the birds I saw. Huge great bustards, feathers ruffled, stooping in the corner of a rapeseed field. An encounter with a Eurasian stone-curlew, a brown, long-legged bird with eyes like golden saucers, which is almost invisible in tall grass. In the park in Debrecen a Syrian woodpecker, which at that time was still a rarity in Poland, though today it excites little interest. And also sapphire-blue rollers perching on every telegraph wire along the road as they hunted for prey. In the mid-nineties the roller population in Poland was in crisis; today, two decades later, they are close to extinction here.

A year later we went to Scandinavia. Once again I have no recollection of the people or towns. The latter, in fact, we avoided deliberately. From the journey through Oslo I remember only the barnacle geese in the city park. What stuck in my mind were spruce forests, branches entwined with beard-like lichens, dwarf birches, moss cushions of many colours. And the birds. Willow ptarmigan concealed in the tundra; a solitary loon on a lake amid a melancholy wilderness. The rocky cliffs of the island of Runde and the penguin-like auks that were poor fliers – the pictures from page 130 had finally come to life.

The Danube delta. On the way, Transylvanian houses roofed with corrugated iron, packs of stray dogs wherever we stopped. Our Polish bus from Przemyśl with a rusty hole in its right side and a fan belt that broke on a difficult ascent. At our destination there was basically nothing but nature. Swallows flew into the campground café through the open window, swooped over the tables and disappeared into nests hanging high on the walls. The natural world didn't rest even in the night-time. The grasses were alive with the sound of millions of crickets, like a vast musical instrument improvising in different registers and rhythms. The music of nature doesn't always make sense to the human ear.

Afterwards, on several occasions I had dreams about our boat trip in the delta. Journeys through tunnels of reeds, invisible shortcuts, acres of waterlogged woods. The delta was dominated by plant life. The birds were the guardians of the river country. Massive pelicans, calm and self-assured, passed like light aircraft overhead. Ibises with curved beaks moved through the shallows, glittering metallically. Herons stood poised and motionless on the bank. It was my last family birding trip. I was gradually beginning to need independence.

Bird books are written in a particular language. Even as a child I became sufficiently familiar with them so that professional terminology held no mysteries for me. They were pure meaning without style; I didn't notice their comic potential. It was strange, since in my school compositions I would choose my words carefully. I soon realised that, despite what the Polish teachers told us, it was sometimes better to repeat a word than strain for an unwieldy synonym. I wasn't going to substitute the word 'bird' with some clumsy alternative like 'winged wanderer'.

It must be said that the language of bird books can seem ungainly to someone who has always liked to read. Yet at the same time their vocabulary can't be replaced with neutral, everyday language. The words used in guides are precise and appropriate: male, female, nourishment, feeding. It's hard to argue with the fact that birds don't eat like people – that they're not gentlemen and ladies. To transfer ideas unthinkingly from the world of human concepts to animals is to lapse into infantilism. Birds don't make love, go to bed, or even have sex. They copulate. This technical term conveys the essence of the matter. There's no romance here; it's purely a question of reproduction and of passing on one's genes. Copulation. The activity can't be called anything else.

Such words are in fact familiar to anyone who has studied biology, or watched a nature documentary. But there's also another, less obvious vocabulary. Every part of a bird's body and every component of its plumage has its own name. A Polish term for plumage is '*szata*', meaning 'gown' or 'robes' – I'm especially fond of that word, which to an outsider is redolent of incense and Sunday Scripture readings. Plumage depends on age, season and the bird's sex. It can be fresh or old. Each species has different plumages and changes them (through moulting) in a particular sequence.

Words taken from descriptions of the human figure are curious. In one guide I found the adjective 'broad-shouldered'. Yet it wasn't used to describe some imposing, powerful species. Eagles don't always have broad shoulders. Birds are often described in contrast to similar species. It's usually a matter of subtle differences in proportion, a fleeting impression that's hard to pinpoint. Thus, in Lars Jonsson's guide the wood warbler is said to be 'more broad-shouldered' than the willow warbler, which it closely resembles. I once read this description to some friends, and for a moment I couldn't understand why they laughed. It's enough to glance at these two birds, each measuring just over ten centimetres, to realise that we're not talking about human broad-shoulderedness here.

The same is true of 'facial expression'. Birds of course do not have faces in our understanding of the word, but the juxtaposition of various lines, brows, bright and dark patches on the head can give the impression of features and emotions. A striking example is a pair of closely related birds that are the smallest species in Europe: the goldcrest and the firecrest. The former has a bright patch around its eye, which gives it a pleasant, innocent appearance. The firecrest looks like its evil twin brother. Beneath its broad white eyebrow is a demonic black line that passes through the coal-black eye. A grey mark underneath the eye completes the picture. This little creature, which weighs six grams, looks as if it hasn't slept well in days.

The terms used to indicate one's chance of seeing a given species are intriguing. 'Common' does not at all mean ordinary, banal, uninteresting. A species is common if its population is numerous. An 'occasional visitor', in turn, is a bird whose migratory routes do not generally pass through the specified territory, but which does occasionally stray that way. 'Vagrant' is something quite different – a true rarity. It comes by once in a blue moon, usually by chance, for example when it is blown to land by a storm. I also like 'invasive'. Such birds are unpredictable. One winter they'll appear here in great numbers, then a year later there'll be no more than a handful.

Ryszard Kapuściński once wrote this poem:

> ... The grey wagtail
> has lovely plumage
> a black throat
> dark brown wings
> black bill
>
> it lives by streams
> it is known for its animation
> and its perpetual song
> tsissis
> tsissis
> tsier
> tsissis ...

The poem's epigraph comes from another Polish poet of the same generation, Edward Stachura: 'All is poetry.'

By the end of primary school I had a fairly good knowledge of birds, but I was less and less interested in reading about them. When I started high school, I began to discover the advantages of reduced parental control. I continued going birdwatching, but it was more along the lines of an involuntary reflex. I repeated the activities I'd learnt to do over the years, but automatically, ever more rarely and without enjoyment. My excitement was fading away.

After my first year of high school I talked the two Michałs, my best friends, into going on a trip to northern Scandinavia with me. It was still supposedly a birding expedition, but entirely unlike the previous ones. We drank watery Finnish beer till we passed out; we clambered up weathered sea cliffs, did some small-scale shoplifting from a roadside store. The chill of fear and the thrill of mischief became the measure of whether we were having fun. The birds took a back seat, though I was still capable of being stunned at the sight of golden plover by the pale light of the subarctic night.

My friends weren't that interested in birds, but it didn't matter. The freedom and a generous amount of pocket money were sufficiently enticing that the following year the three of us went to Corsica and Sardinia. In the intervening period we'd been avidly acquiring drinking experiences, so this time we weren't brought to our knees by any old stuff. We thought we were adults. We walked fearlessly into Corsican bars where a dozen or so men would be singing some mournful tune. They were drinking and their eyes were glassy. They paid no attention to us whatsoever. I can't even remember whether I managed to see the Corsican nuthatch endemic to the island during the course of those two weeks.

Birds slipped lower and lower on my list of priorities. I even stopped taking my binoculars on trips. It was rare that a bird sighting could stop me in my tracks. After our last year of high school Michał B. and I travelled to the Ukrainian Carpathians. Just the two of us. A true manly adventure. From that first visit to Ukraine I remember mostly fear – the impression that everyone was lying in wait to kill us and that they were all in cahoots. The fact that we could barely read Cyrillic did not help matters.

Our inability to communicate led to some ridiculous situations. I spent ten minutes in a shop refusing 'vodichka', thinking that the shameless woman was plying me with some kind of vodka, when actually she was trying to give me water. Ukrainians in fact call vodka *gorilka*, but we didn't know that then. A nice guy with an array of gold teeth, who chatted with us in the train, seemed highly suspicious to us. We waited with bated breath for him to hold us up. At the end of our first day, exhausted by these experiences, I was genuinely pleased to see a three-toed woodpecker that was blithely ignoring us as it patrolled a spruce trunk directly outside our tent.

Yet I stuck with Ukraine. I filled my passport with stamps from different border crossings: Rava Rus'ka, Yahodyn, Shehyni, Mostyska. Then a couple of years later I revisited familiar places in the Danube delta. During clumsy negotiations with the fishermen who rented out boats I realised I could understand their private conversation. They were descendants of Zaporozhian Cossacks whose ancestors, driven out of the

Sich by Catherine II, had settled in these parts. They spoke an archaic language that I knew from a nineteenth-century parody of *The Aeneid* by Ivan Kotlyarevsky, the father of Ukrainian literature. The pelicans in the river wetlands were just as stately, the herons as immobile as ever. Yet my abiding memory of the trip was that Ukrainian enclave in the marshes.

Reading the transcription of a bird's call in a toneless voice is always good for a laugh. 'Kyowkyowkyowkyowkyowkkighkyah', Sokołowski has the herring gull cry. In Svensson's guide it emits 'its well-known exalted courtship laugh': 'kiyaaa-kiya-kiya-kiya-kiya-kiya-kiya-kiya-kiyow'. It's no small feat to capture the subtle rhythm and tenor of a call. Try conveying a soccer referee's whistle using the letters of the alphabet. Unadorned onomatopoeia is awkward, but combined with an apt description it can give a good idea of the sound.

'Evenly, in an unhurried rhythm the flutelike tones come soft and sweet, slightly sorrowful like a lullaby, but most agreeable. This song is one of the pleasantest of all. It can be conveyed rather well thus: "lululu lyul dyil dyil lilili," and so on. The woodlark's song must have come to people's attention long ago, for there are numerous folk names that imitate its sound, for example Firlej, Ledwucha, Filuszka, Suliszka. Closest of all, though, is the Latin name *Lullula*,' we read in *Birds of the Polish Lands*. The author, Jan Sokołowski, loved such folk interpretations of song. The great reed warbler, for example, sings as follows:

Ribber ribber ribber,
rack rack rack,
swishty swishty swishty,
drab drab drab,
starry starry starry,
kit kit kit.

These days thousands of high-quality recordings can be found online. But birdsong has been an inspiration in every era. People have attempted to write it down with musical notes, letters of the alphabet, ingenious diagrams. Scientists, poets, and musicians have tried their hand. A well-known anecdote claims that the beginning of Beethoven's Fifth Symphony was suggested by an ortolan bunting that the composer overheard. Vivaldi wrote a flute concerto called 'The Goldfinch'. Olivier Messiaen was inspired by the dawn chorus he heard in the trenches of the Second World War when creating *Quartet for the End of Time*. The work premiered on 15 January 1941 in Stalag VIIIA at Görlitz (today's Zgorzelec in Poland), where the composer was a prisoner of war.

I myself am endlessly fascinated by the early sixteenth-century polyphonic songs of Clément Janequin. Their author, a Catholic priest who towards the end of his life was appointed 'composer ordinary' to the King, wrote several works incorporating birdsong. His best-known song – 'Le chant des oiseaux' – celebrates the miracle of nature reawakening in the spring. Our hearts fill with joy at the sounds of the song thrush, the nightingale and also the 'treacherous' cuckoo. The performers imitate in song the trills, whistles, and twitterings:

'Frian, frian, frian, frian, frian, frian, frian, frian; ticun, ticun, ticun, ticun, ticun, ticun; qui la ra, qui la ra, qui la ra; huit, huit, huit, huit, huit, huit, huit, huit, huit…'

Towards the end of my college years my ornithological seismograph recorded several major tremors. In a bookstore I came across a new Polish version of Lars Jonsson's *Birds of Europe*. I couldn't resist, though I already owned the English edition, bought at considerable cost in London. I'd long known about the Polish translation, and as I leafed through the book I knew I had to have it. At that time it was the best field guide, before it was surpassed by the practical, comprehensive Collins.

Jonsson is no ordinary guidebook. I see it rather as a work of art. The author's illustrations are precise, yet at the same time they exude artistic panache. I'm captivated by their artful detail, the melding of colours, the glints of light, the meticulous technique. The extraordinary feeling for movement, for initial impression. '[E]very depiction of a bird is basically an interpretation and [...] can convey only a certain part of the complex reality, no matter how intimately the bird has been studied,' the author writes in the introduction. In his interpretations, however, he does not seek the simplest solutions; he places his subjects in atypical poses and employs bravura foreshortenings. The bill of a shoveller staring at the reader is magnificent.

A good illustration in a guide book ought to show the bird accurately and in as much detail as possible. Most illustrators therefore omit the background or include it only where absolutely necessary. A woodpecker has to be seen gripping a tree trunk. But the other birds are usually abstracted from their environment and placed in a neutral, uniform plane. In Jonsson's book, it's the backgrounds that I like best. They're simplified, sometimes barely sketched, at other times given depth; they're interesting in their own right and seem to share equal billing with the birds.

Jonsson's backgrounds are almost palpable. Dry, thorny scrub littered with snail shells; brittle cup lichen on the branches. The author shows the birds in context, in their natural environment. A bearded reedling on a palisade of reeds; a scops owl with its yellow eye almost lost against the bark of an olive tree. He captures colour brilliantly too: the hazy watercolour blue of the northern seas, or the clay-green of an autumn field. He renders even the most conventional scene dynamic. A female bullfinch pecks at some casually sketched fruit. Blackberries? They're so simplified that they seem unnecessary, yet it's thanks to them that the illustration comes to life.

An appreciation for Jonsson's work, however, did not make me want to snatch up my binoculars and leave the house. It was an aesthetic experience. It happened a few times that I would spend a whole evening looking through the book, but I still did not regain my enthusiasm for going birding. I preferred the birds to come to me. While I was living in the country writing my master's thesis I kept a notebook of sightings. For two weeks I listed only those birds that I saw from my window, which looked on to a grove of birch trees. It came to forty-one species.

I resumed birding seriously a few years ago and eagerly went about making up for lost time. I began by buying new binoculars. I was as pleased as punch. I peeked into neighbouring apartments, excitedly read distant licence plates. I chose a model with a classic design, nitrogen-filled, resistant to steaming, and thus more durable. A good piece of equipment, though maybe a little on the heavy side. These days I'd buy a pair with less magnification, but handier and more versatile.

Next I bought the aforementioned guide by Lars Svensson ('the Collins'), a fat little volume filled with brilliantly condensed information. The illustrations perhaps lacked finesse, but they captured the characteristic features of the various species. The language was not to be sniffed at either. Likening the profile of a great grey owl to a steamship ventilator may seem a bit of a stretch, but it indicates a quest for new kinds of description that are less technical and appeal more to the imagination. And he's on to something with his daring comparison of an owl's outline to part of a ship.

I began too to meet new people, join groups, go on tours with other birders. I leapt into birding with the zeal of a neophyte. I spent every spring weekend outdoors, I followed the birding reports from around the country. As the owner of an old but functioning car I could count on being popular. The last time I met so many people linked by a single goal was in high school. Then, it was the need to study; now it was a shared hobby. It turned out that this passion changes you for good. You don't always have to be tramping through woods and marshes, but your eye will always be drawn by a woodpecker flying past. You'll never be indifferent to the glossy beauty of the first starlings of spring. You'll always halt at the sound of an unfamiliar call. You'll never stop watching.

CHEŁMOŃSKI'S HAWK

LATE AUTUMN, YET THE MEADOWS seen from the bluff still look green. Apparently cranes gather here in the evenings, but at nine in the morning I see only some deer scampering about amid the hay bundles. I come back after sundown. I search for the cranes by sound: every couple of hundred metres I cut the engine and listen. I follow a pair of birds for a minute, but as they approach the ground they disappear beyond the willow beds till I can no longer hear their strident clattering. They must have settled somewhere else nearby. More of them fly in soon afterwards; this time I don't try to give chase, but only watch them to the point when they land.

When nothing's left of the sun but a pink afterglow, the sodden grass turns grey. There are no clouds; a mild night is setting in. I walk towards a spilled hay bundle, the only hiding place on the mown meadow. When I'm ten feet away, the hay moves, and a startled deer emerges. It eyes me for a moment, then runs off. Every few metres it leaps high, like an African antelope. The hay is warm. I make myself comfortable in it and I see a whole flock – there must be a hundred cranes. They're not standing in silence but rather squeaking, gurgling, hooting. On the meadow I can also hear the muttering of snipe; from time to time one of them rises up and passes me in its zigzag flight. Through the binoculars the image is still clear. I see the long bill, then the bird melts into the darkness.

Eleven more cranes fly in from the east. They call from high up and at once receive a response from the meadow. Permission to land has been granted. The birds wheel in a tight circle and drop steeply downwards. They lower their legs like landing gear before they touch down. In my blurred photograph they look like giant mosquitoes. More birds appear in the dark sky. And again those on the ground invite the new arrivals to land. There is a hierarchy: the least prestigious spots are at the edge of the flock. There it's easiest to be eaten; you have to keep an eye out, watch for danger. The worthiest individuals have places in the centre.

The cranes settle down and, for a few minutes, I hear only the soft croaking of one bird or another. Most have put their head under a wing. Then all of a sudden there's a commotion. Ten cranes fly off, honking in indignation. A moment later, after reflection, another dozen or so join them. It's as if one bird, dissatisfied with the location assigned to it, had complained to the hosts and then left in a huff with its family. A disgruntled crane and its loyal relatives. Then later, more hesitantly, its friends. The secessionists come to earth in a neighbouring field. Cranes apparently have complex social relations, but I don't know if they're easily offended and oversensitive about their own dignity.

The deer no longer care – they're wandering about a few metres from me. Night is falling; the elegant blue of the sky gradually darkens. In the silence there's a crash, and a red flash of lightning cuts horizontally across the air. Only human beings act so indecorously, I decide. In the darkness, frightened ducks fly past with a quacking and a scurry of wings. Somewhere close by there's the thud of small hooves, but I can no longer see the deer's white rumps bobbing up and down. I don't want to be mistaken for a wild boar sleeping in the hay, and so I slowly take my leave.

I've always had a fondness for the painter Józef Chełmoński and the unadorned, living nature seen in his paintings. 'He had an extraordinary memory for form and movement, immense sensitivity, and a capacity for direct, intimate contact with nature,' wrote art historian Jan Wegner. His ability revealed itself early, though those first canvases, conventional and colouristically bland, were not especially promising. In 1870, at the age of twenty-one, he exhibited *Departure of the Cranes*, a sombre autumn landscape with a flock of cranes rising into flight. Chełmoński depicted the cranes at different phases of their flight: some of them are already vanishing in the morning mist, others are just taking off. The scene is being observed by a solitary, motionless bird with one wing hanging inertly. For it the journey is over. The spirit of the picture is already that of the modernist movement Young Poland, or perhaps it's still Romantic? It's melancholy, unsettling. The work is admired. Critics write that the painter 'captures the truth with ease'.

What of it: Chełmoński, a student of Wojciech Gerson, lives in poverty for many years after. Friends arrange meals for him in a canteen, from which he brings home slices of bread concealed in his pockets. But he's determined. He acquires a horse's leg from a butcher's shop and studies it in such detail that his room fills with the stench of rotting flesh. His fellow tenants force him to throw his model away.

In 1871 he leaves for Munich, where there's a sizeable colony of Polish artists. There are people there he can learn from. For instance Józef Brandt, who has a fascination with Cossacks; the battle-scene painter Juliusz Kossak; and the brilliant Maksymilian Gierymski (who will, alas, die young). Many of the artists have lived through the January Uprising, and perhaps for that reason their works often contain grey uniforms and flat, mournful landscapes. But Chełmoński isn't comfortable in Munich; he misses Poland and its familiar scenery. He's moved by an abandoned garden, overgrown with nettles, that he comes upon by chance. In a letter to his teacher Gerson he laments: 'In Poland things are different, different, different.' In 1873 he paints *A Case Before the Village Headman*. The thatched cottage and the crowd in traditional clothing mark the beginning of a whole series of images in 'blacks, browns, ochres, greys, ashen whites, faded greens and blues, with judicious accents in red or yellow'.

He moves to Paris, and it's only now that he establishes himself. His paintings are bought by leading dealers; art collectors are charmed by his wintry landscapes and the weather-beaten faces of the peasants of the Mazowsze region. Chełmoński begins to paint with the tastes of his buyers in mind. He repeats popular motifs to exhaustion. His friends worry that he's frittering away his talent. But in 1886 he creates the magnificent *Bustards*. 'A dull, greenish, chaotic canvas that claims to show bustards on the steppe, though in essence it depicts nothing,' the art critic of the magazine *Kłosy* writes disapprovingly.

It's early morning. Autumnal grass rimed in hoarfrost. A flock of sodden bustards is resting in the mist. They sit on the ground, cleaning their feathers. Superbly observed detail is combined with a naturalness in the birds' forms. Bustards are skittish creatures; how did Chełmoński manage to get close to them? And the *Kłosy* critic is mistaken: this is not at all the steppe. The artist's daughter Wanda recalled that her father had observed the birds at Meudon, close to Versailles. Nor is it true that the painting 'depicts nothing' – its subject is nature undisturbed by humans and human-made objects.

Bustards was painted in two versions. The later, better-known one hangs in the National Museum in Warsaw. A second, lighter one, with a distinctive upright figure of a bird on the lookout, can be seen at the Chełmoński Museum in Radziejowice. *Bustards*, though, is the exception amid dozens of identical-looking horse-drawn carts, sleighs sinking into wet snow, peasant women in red headscarves, and peasant men in fur hats. In 1887 Chełmoński gives up hack work and returns to Poland. Two years later he buys a manor house built of larchwood in the village of Kuklówka in Mazowsze.

At times the tired glow of evening is uncannily like the blush of an early morning sky. Yet it isn't the same light. I had planned to be in place while it was still completely dark, but I was waylaid by the lure of watery coffee from a petrol station. A harrier emerges silently out of the dim light behind me and glides across the meadow one metre from the ground. In the spilled hay bundle is the impression of the deer's body. But there's no sign of the cranes. Maybe they're roosting on the ground, and they'll only rise at dawn? The wet grass is still ashen with hoarfrost in the shadows. Snipe fly up from under my feet, resentfully calling 'kshick, kshick'. Somewhere close by I hear the familiar sounds: the cranes are on the other side of an overgrown drainage canal. I can't jump over it in wellington boots, with my binoculars. And in November I'm not crazy about the prospect of wading through dark water. I have to find a way around.

Amid ideally shaped sleeping bags of hay the deer are grazing calmly. Now and again they raise their heads and give me the once-over. I seem not to smell of danger, and my binoculars don't resemble a shotgun, so after a moment they go back to munching the grass. In the early morning mist the sunlight surrounds me on all sides. I follow pathways made by the animals; I can hear that the cranes are very close. Another dark, stagnant canal appears in my way. If it weren't there, the meadow would be flooded all year round. The birds probably wouldn't object. The murmur of their voices now separates into individual whistling and bubbling sounds. A couple of steps on tiptoe and suddenly I see their bright, elongated figures among the dried stalks. A flock at least a hundred strong is resting behind the reeds. My camera's autofocus is baffled by the curtain of rushes.

I take a step forward and I sense I've been noticed. That's that; they'll all fly off any moment now. There's a tense pause beyond the reeds; I try to retreat, but I place my foot clumsily and a twig snaps. For a second there's silence, then the entire flock rises with a deafening cry. I squat down in hopes that the birds will just circle around and return. But no: they leave for good. There are 200 or more. To begin with they fly in disorder, in a huddle, but before long they form an elongated, intricate hieroglyph. Or perhaps it's a full sentence in an unknown alphabet? As a consolation, a few metres from me two bright blue kingfishers speed past with a piercing screech. One of them perches on a dry stalk, exactly like the one in the little painting by Van Gogh.

Daybreak; small pink clouds, and birds erect in the first rays of the sun. The cranes are somewhat against the light, so they seem darker than in reality. There's only a faint contrast between the white strip behind their eye and their red skullcap. There, on the meadows along the Noteć River, I had wanted to see a live version of 1910's *Greeting the Sun*.

After returning to Poland, Chełmoński changes his style radically. He sets aside horse-drawn carts and peasant gatherings in snow-covered thatched cottages. He abandons the subject matter that brought him fame and fortune. He even changes his palette: over the years his images become brighter, more gentle. At Kuklówka he paints almost exclusively landscapes and animals. After his divorce he becomes a little quirky and falls prey to religious mania.

Pia Górska, the daughter of neighbours and a student of Chełmoński's, left us an interesting account of him. The first time she saw the master, he was weeping as he prayed during Mass. 'There was a diffidence and a mistrustfulness in him that made contact with other people hard.' Chełmoński abruptly breaks off a visit he's making because he wants to go back to a stork he left at home. He tells strange, rambling stories that lead nowhere. These anecdotes create an image of the kind of person often diplomatically called eccentric. He's awkward in his social relations, but great people are forgiven such trifles. Pia, her parents, the neighbours, the local peasants – in a word, everyone – are all convinced that Chełmoński is an exceptional individual.

'I write this plain-spoken, unliterary memoir for two reasons,' Pia writes in the introduction to her book. 'First, I like to talk and think about Chełmoński. Second, I believe that few people have had the privilege of spending time with a person of such outstanding calibre, and it's said that privilege should not be wasted.' During one of Chełmoński's visits to the Górskis at their village of Wola Pękoszewska his photograph was taken. A bearded man stares absently into the distance. One hand rests on his side, the other props up his neck. It's not a studied pose, but an authentic testament to pensiveness.

'You see a dew-covered field, miss,' he explains to Pia. 'It seems like nothing at all, yet it's very hard to depict that drabness. People are idiots! They think that only those praying on their knees serve God, whereas I say that painting a dewy field like that is also a service to God, maybe even better than another.' The painter wanders the neighbourhood on foot in a peasant straw hat. He studies the appearance of plants, bird behaviour, glints of sunlight, the colour of grass in the spring and of leaves in the autumn. He has an astounding memory. He examines things in detail. He makes pencil sketches of waterfowl which he captions expertly: 'merganser', 'tufted duck', 'northern pintail', 'scaup'. In 1891 he paints a picture titled *The Bittern*, showing a bird flying over a flooded meadow, with its camouflage plumage painstakingly detailed. The canvas is compositionally straightforward – the principal subject, placed centrally, and the waterlogged terrain. The sky has no particular colour; it's perhaps the middle of the day. There are no dramatic underlit cloudlets. Nothing attracts especial attention. Everything is in the title.

The same year Chełmoński produces *Partridges in the Snow*, one of his most famous paintings. Here too the title says it all. The hungry, anxious birds move across a snowy wilderness in a tight-knit bunch. Reproductions usually fail to preserve the subtle half-tones. One bird is looking about warily. The horizon dissolves in a pale grey mist that virtually blends into the colour of the sky. And, once again, the details. The ruddy smudge on the wing coverts of the birds closest to the viewer; the stooping figures in the middle distance melting into the haze. Mature Chełmoński is regarded as being on the borderline between realism and symbolism – the partridges in the snow are said to be us, oppressed by the hardships of life. What I see here above all, though, is close observation and a profound understanding of nature. There's no need to exalt an already outstanding painting and burden it with additional significance.

Chełmoński paints *The Moorhen*, *Lapwings*, *Hunting Capercaillie*. *The Jay*, a bird in wintertime scattering white dust from a snow-covered pine. In 1899 comes *The Hawk: Fair Weather*. It's like an illustration to the lines from Adam

Mickiewicz's epic poem *Pan Tadeusz*: 'Elsewhere a hawk flutters its wings up high / Looking just like a pinned-down butterfly.' Chełmoński adored Mickiewicz. It's no disparagement of the genius of either the great poet or the great artist if I say that the two of them are dealing with different species. Mickiewicz's bird is probably a buzzard or kestrel: both hover over meadows in search of prey. Chełmoński's creature is most likely a hobby: dark head, narrow wings and red undertail. Birds of prey are rarely seen up close; it's hardly surprising that for the majority of people they remain forever 'hawks'.

I arrive in Kuklówka after seven in the morning on a rather gloomy day one hot summer. The clouds seem determined to finally break and send down long-expected rain. An avenue of trees offers a clear indication of where to look for the manor house, which is itself not visible from the road. But signs say: 'Private Road', 'Farm, Private Property'. I walk around the modest grounds; two mongrels are yapping amid magnificent oaks and lindens. Fallen leaves rustle indiscreetly underfoot. To the right is a field of golden stubble. At the far end of the grounds there's a clearing that slopes gently away towards an alder grove. Somewhere down there amid the trees is a small river called Pisia Tuczna.

I sit at the edge of the clearing and watch a flycatcher, which is waiting in the low branches of an oak for passing flies. It darts up, hangs for a moment in the air, then returns to its perch. I go through species in my mind. From high up comes the croak of a

A hobby out hunting

raven; cranes are calling in the distance. An unseen woodpecker drums vehemently on a tree. The sound seems too loud, out of place in this sultry stillness, like an older person hammering away at a computer keyboard. Just when I'm about to get up, two young fawns run out from the alders. For a while they chase about the meadow as children will; a cautious doe stands by the trees scanning the area. I freeze and watch the scene at the edge of Chełmoński's estate.

The deer vanish only when a young boy appears on the horizon leading a bull. The creature protests, though it sounds as if it's been gagged: 'Mmmmm, mmm, mmmmm.' The metallic clank of a stake being driven into the ground, and a moment later the bull is trimming the grass. The boy leaves without looking in my direction. A few drops of rain fall. I walk back along the lane to my car. I parked by a stone which the inhabitants of Kuklówka erected in honour of 'The Great Painter of the Polish Countryside'. A ruddy tail juts up from the asphalt. It's all that's left of a run-over squirrel, like a little monument marking its death.

'Nature spoke to his responsive mind in all the variety of its manifestations; he was fascinated not only by form, colour, and light! He strove to express the music of the evening, the whisper of a bat's wings, the quiet flight of nightjars, the croaking of frogs, the corncrake's grating call, and the far-off boom of the bittern... He was the first, perhaps the only painter to depict a swarm of mosquitoes buzzing in the air, and the hum of a cockchafer speeding past like a bullet. He wanted the wind in his pictures to whistle through the dried sunflower stalks, to make the rain patter on the window pane, and set the bucket on the well-sweep clanking … He made paintings in which the distant ringing of the mail bell was meant to carry through the thick fog, resound moaningly across the steppe dozing in the haze, and wake the wet, sleepy bustards.' Thus Chełmoński's friend and fellow artist Stanisław Witkiewicz wrote about him.

1898. Two stately swans sail across the waters of *The Pond at Radziejowice*. On the far side can be glimpsed the tower of the small castle of the Krasińskis, an important family in Poland's military and artistic history. It is faint in the morning mist, but already lit by the rays of the sun. Today that castle, or rather the stately home adjoining it, houses the Józef Chełmoński Museum. The whole property is beautifully maintained. On the balcony a young couple pose for a photograph. In the museum I'm sort of shooed away: 'Come back in ten minutes, on the hour,' then I'm made to hang around for a long time while the lady in the ticket office finishes her conversation. She's explaining to someone that Polish pianists come here to practise for the Chopin Piano Competition, under the supervision of American teachers. Everyone walks around on tiptoe. I have to wait in the first room for someone to take me upstairs.

I sit by an unlit lamp and gaze at the slushy roads in *In Front of the Inn* from 1877. In this dark room the springtime emptiness of the painting is even more lugubrious. Hanging next to it is *Bustards*. From close up, the bird sitting on the ground is flashing its golden eye at me. The lady who leads me up the stairs reminds me that I shouldn't dawdle because I have to complete my visit within the hour. From behind a door a Chopin nocturne plays, while I look at *Good Friday*. *In Front of the Inn* now seems quite cheerful by comparison. There at least there was the drunken crowd, the old man dancing, the peasant women in their red headscarves. Here, on the other hand, is the dim light of a new moon, the deathly stillness of dry stalks on a russet-red meadow. And that dour procession heading for the church. The audio guide speaks repeatedly in lofty tones of 'an emotion-filled reverie'.

Marsh Marigolds: Spring from 1908. Bright, filled with light, like most of the late pictures. A May meadow, yellow as can be, a broad clear sky, and 'a pair of storks that bring calm to the picture', as the voice in the headphones explains. A glance at the birds' broad, rounded wings and short dark necks is enough to ascertain that they're not storks. Art historians don't worry overmuch about identifying species. The black-and-white forms are lapwings tumbling in the air. Anyone who has once seen their crazed display flight knows that it's diametrically opposed to the stork's dignified glide. The lapwing, with its airborne acrobatics, is the springtime apotheosis of life and vitality. In Chełmoński there are no chance birds. He always painted particular species in a carefully chosen setting and in perfectly depicted motion.

I go by Kuklówka one more time. I wanted to emulate Chełmoński, study the blue stars of chicory in the meadow, but I really should take a look at the house. The stubble field is patrolled by a sparrowhawk being mobbed by a swarm of shrill swallows. The dogs give the alarm, a woman comes out, and I explain that I wouldn't have forgiven myself if I hadn't come for a look. Her broad, inviting gesture tells me I'm not the first to have done so. The manor is rather hut-like, with a gable roof and a glassed-in porch, a small upper storey on the garden side. The dark larchwood warms in the afternoon sun. The garden overlooks the alder grove; beyond it is a huge, ugly, orange house. The woman guesses my thoughts. She says: 'Chełmoński saw something entirely different. Before, there were ponds here. He could walk out of the house and right away paint those moorhens of his.'

A SAP-SCENTED COAL TIT

TOWARDS THE END OF SUMMER, when their young are already reared, swallows abandon their nests on the walls of houses and gather into flocks. They hold assemblies on telephone wires, and in the evenings they fill the reed beds with their shrill chatter. Then one morning they disappear. For centuries people wondered what happened to these birds, which vanished from one day to the next, only to turn up again in the spring. There were numerous theories. Aristotle thought that swallows and hawks hide from the cold in caves, then fly back out when they're woken by the warmth of springtime. It was suspected that the cuckoo changes into a sparrowhawk for the winter. (Was it because the two species have a similar blueish tinge to their plumage and distinctive bars on the breast?)

Olaus Magnus, the sixteenth-century Archbishop of Uppsala, was convinced that swallows don't fly away at all, but plunge underwater directly from the reed beds where they spend their nights. Once down there they form tight huddles, bird by bird, wing by wing, and await the coming of spring. When the weather gets warmer, they emerge from the water and set about rebuilding their nests. It apparently happened that fishermen would find torpid birds in the water in winter. The wiser ones would throw them back, believing that a swallow that warmed up would fly away, but after a short while would drop dead. For whatever reason, the archbishop's theory remained persuasive for a long time. The English anatomist John Hunter enclosed swallows in an orangery lined with reeds, with a large tub of water in the middle. Strangely, the birds did not even go near the tub. In 1773 Italian scholars experimented to see how long swallows could exist underwater. As it turned out, not very long.

Yet it was already known that birds migrate. As early as the mid-thirteenth century, in his *On the Art of Hunting with Birds*, the German Emperor Frederick II wrote about migration in a strikingly informed manner. He understood that it was connected with the cycle of the seasons, with the cold that came in the autumn, and the difficulty of finding food. He knew that some birds migrate along the coasts and some by river valleys, and that certain birds fly by night, others during the daylight hours. He had also observed that certain species migrate in flocks, others fly alone. If he was already aware of these things, why was it that 500 years later scientists were still drowning swallows?

In Podlasie, eastern Poland, the snow is knee-deep; in Warsaw there's melting slush; while Pomorze on the Baltic coast has the colour of waterlogged fields and last year's grass. It's a little as if late November had made a comeback. Deer splash about the open space, along with far-from-timid cranes. The bus to the north-western coastal village of Dąbki is completely empty; the melancholy of off-season resorts. Half the shops are closed; the amusements – beat-up, coin-operated red cars and pink ponies with music boxes attached – are frozen in hibernation. The sun behind the trees throws shadows on the road like Venetian blinds, but it doesn't yet provide any warmth. A dazzling white flock of swans passes across the intense blue sky.

A robin is in the net. He stares at me in silence, resigned to what he believes is the coming end. Only occasionally does he try to peck at his persecutor, though his beak, a tiny little thing used for catching small insects, makes no impression at all on a human hand. A great spotted woodpecker is another proposition. It struggles with all its might, furiously, contemptuous of death. Its powerful claws penetrate skin as easily and deeply as curved needles. It strikes at fingers with its blunt bill the way it hammers on wood, causing shallow but painful wounds. And the entire time it screeches, screeches, in fear and anger. Or take tits, for instance. They don't look like much, but they administer nasty nips to the fingertips and the tender skin of the hand. They infallibly find the most sensitive places.

For these reasons, a meek little robin is good to start off with. Such a lesson in patience. 'Taking a bird out of the net is like taking a cardigan off a small child,' Justyna says. You hold the bird with one hand, with the other you pull away the threads, and the wings yield to your actions. Work decisively, but carefully. Mind the delicate legs, thinner than matchsticks, with the rough, light-coloured foot at the end. Hold the joints still. The leg is the frailest part of the robin. The bird is not your collaborator, you won't convince it to play along. It'll always try to break free. You pull in one direction while it thrashes blindly, entangling itself more and more in the holes of the net.

According to legend, the first proof of bird migrations was brought in 1250 by a swallow to whose leg some Cistercian monks had previously attached a piece of parchment with a message. The bird had supposedly flown back with a reply from Asia. An almost identical story is alleged to have taken place in Poland. A certain member of the gentry hung a little sign around a stork's neck with the proud inscription: *Haec ciconia ex Polonia* (This stork is from Poland). In the spring, he received the courteous response: *India cum donis remittit ciconiam Polonis* (India sends the Poles their stork back with gifts).

It sometimes happened that, when birds were caught during a hunt but were otherwise unharmed, a ring would be placed around their leg with the date and the hunter's coat of arms. In 1677 King John III Sobieski is said to have trapped a heron that thirty years earlier King Ladislaus IV had held in his hands. Similar incidents occurred elsewhere in Europe. The heron was released to glorify the name of the Polish king; no one had yet thought of studying its habits. Rings were put on out of boredom too. One famous case was that of an aristocrat who, in hiding from the bloody-thirsty during the French Revolution, put a copper ring on the leg of a swallow. Apparently the bird returned to the same place each year for three years.

The eccentric Danish teacher Hans Christian Cornelius Mortensen is regarded as the father of modern ringing. Ornithologist and writer Niels Otto Preuss recounts that Mortensen wrote his notes on small yellow cards sewn together, to save on notebooks. The colour yellow, Mortensen claimed, is less tiring on the eyes. He placed the first zinc bands on the legs of two starlings in 1890. Yet they proved to be too heavy. Mortensen switched from zinc to aluminium, and inscribed 'Viborg' (the name of the city where he lived and conducted his experiments) and successive numbers on the rings. He placed them in small tins filled with sand. His students had to carry these tins in their pockets so the heavy grains would polish the sharp edges of the bands. Using boxes with a mechanism that closed automatically, he captured and ringed 165 starlings. Over the following years he did the same with birds of various species. Soon other scientists were taking an interest in Mortensen's method. In 1903, the first station for researching bird migrations was established at Rossitten on the Curonian Spit.

When you're in the canteen tent ordinary rain feels like a downpour. The drops strike against the taut canvas as if hitting a drum; the sound resonates and soon turns into an unbroken din. When it rains, rounds are conducted twice as frequently as usual. Haste is needed. When birds perch on a branch in the rain, they tuck their head under their shoulder and the raindrops run off their covert feathers like off a raincoat. They wait out the rain. But in the net it's different. When they try to free themselves as they hang upside down or on their back, they're like a person drowning in an icy sea. The feathers on their belly soak up water like a compress, their body cools, and they instantly weaken.

My wren has become horribly snarled up and, when I kneel down over it, rainwater drips from my sleeves directly onto its body. It's so wet that its feathers look like thinning brown hair under which bare skin can be seen. Even if it could break free, it would be incapable of flying away. In the end I manage to disentangle it, and I put it inside my own clothing so it can warm up to the 36.6° centigrade of my body. Before doing so I tuck my shirt into my trousers and cinch my belt so the wren doesn't end up in my underwear. I feel the creature's little claws scraping at my stomach, and the wet bundle moves upwards towards my collar.

The wren is no problem. Drying a tit is more of a challenge; it kicks up a fuss, thrashes about and nips hard with its beak. Extracting a bird from under your clothing, when it has found its way around to your back and crept in under your shoulder blade, is quite a performance. Least troublesome of all is the goldcrest – it perches obediently under your jacket, as close as it can get to the collar. As light as the feathers that cover it – weighing all of five or six grams – at most it expresses its objections with a soft squeak. Its meekness can be fatal. It's been known for someone to forget about the bird under their shirt, then in the evening, as they undress for bed, a stiff little body falls onto the smooth sleeping bag.

To begin with, ringing met with opposition from nature lovers. It was feared that hunters in quest of rings from Rossitten would kill birds in their thousands. (As late as 1959, in his *On the Migrations of Birds*, Zbigniew Swirski writes that rings were collected by 'uncivilised African tribes' as prized amulets.) The German scientists continued their work nevertheless, especially since information about the ringed birds was constantly coming in. By the end of the Second World War about a million birds had been ringed at Rossitten. But during the Russian offensive most of the documentation went up in flames. After the fall of the Reich the station found itself in the Kaliningrad Oblast. It renewed operations in 1956 as the Rybachy Biological Station.

In Poland, for over fifty years birds have been trapped and ringed by the research programme Akcja Bałtycka. It arose in times when the Frontier Guard watched the sea with suspicion. The ploughed-up beaches were patrolled for signs of Swedish spies. Under such conditions, in 1960 a handful of students from Warsaw University spent a month ringing birds that were passing along the Polish coast. The results were sufficiently promising that after only one season the university decided to set up a programme that still exists today. Akcja Bałtycka studies the autumn and spring migrations. The former goes on for a long time, because not all birds are in a hurry to leave for their wintering grounds. After all, many of them don't have far to go and, weather permitting, they remain at home for as long as possible. The spring migration, on the other hand, is a scramble. The birds are in competition for the best territories and the best locations in which to rear their offspring. Ornithological nets cannot be put up in random places, only where the streams of migrating birds are concentrated. For that reason, camps are set up on the narrow isthmus between the sea and Bukowo Lake, on the Vistula Spit, and on the Hel Peninsula. Those are the places through which the birds migrating along the coast have passed for thousands of years on their unchanging airborne highway.

Once the bird is extricated from the net, I put it in a small cotton sack with a drawstring. Some birds are paralysed by fear; others put up uncomplainingly with being transported in this way. There are also those that cry indignantly and try to break out of their imprisonment. Species cannot be combined in the sacks. A tit under duress would immediately kill a goldcrest if the two were accidentally placed together. Thrushes are carried individually, one to a sack. But some birds don't mind company. Outside the breeding season long-tailed tits like to stick together in groups, both in captivity and in the wild. They're netted in loyal company too, several at a time.

I take the birds in the sacks to the ringer. He's in charge of the camp; he decides on the daily schedule, and he's the one who puts the inscribed metal rings on the birds' legs. He also measures and weighs every individual bird caught. I'm a team member. I do the rounds, write down the measurements, follow instructions. The leaders vary, of course. Some rule with an iron hand, others emphasise teamwork. It's a difficult and responsible position: not everyone has charisma or likes giving orders, not everyone functions well under pressure.

It's important to stay calm – during the migration period, every once in a while there comes a minor apocalypse. Especially when there are dramatic changes in the weather, when the birds interrupt their journey and drop to earth in great numbers in the same place. Thousands of them throng a small area. Such a phenomenon is known as a blitz. The woods are filled with a deafening clamour, and birds that are normally cautious and wary are caught in the nets by the hundreds. It's as if they'd lost their reason. The leader has to decide whether the team in camp can manage with emptying the nets. Thanks to well-established procedures there are few casualties. Treecreepers and bullfinches, both highly strung species, have priority in the ringing. Birds that are caught in the net together have to be separated. In such a stressful situation they're capable of pecking at one another. If the number of birds exceeds the capacity of the team, the leader can have the nets taken down until the situation eases.

How do birds know when to migrate? In the summer, when the days get shorter and there's less and less light, their hormones trigger a condition known as migratory restlessness. Caged birds begin to beat against the bars, attempting to fly in their customary direction. First to leave are warmth-loving birds, which have the furthest to go. An internal clock encoded in their genes indicates the right moment. Their sojourn in Poland is short – generally three or four months. It's impossible to imagine an oriole, with its golden feathers, or a sapphire-blue roller, in a snowdrift or in the sleet of March. Short distance flyers like tits and goldcrests set off only when the weather finally makes it difficult for them to find food. They depart when they can no longer put it off. Such species are more resistant to frosts and, since recent winters have increasingly resembled autumn, more and more often they remain where they are.

Species that migrate by night navigate by the stars. Geese and thrushes, for instance, travel this way. During the day they stop to rest and feed. On cloudy nights they pause their journey. Birds that fly by day adjust their path according to the movement of the sun at the horizon. Their brains subconsciously carry out complex calculations – the slightest deviation off course would cause them to miss their destination by hundreds of miles. Some birds recognise landmarks from the air and find their way with stunning accuracy. Young cranes, for instance, set off on their first journey accompanied by their parents – after all, someone older and more experienced has to show them the way.

But that's not all. Tim Birkhead, in his fascinating book *Bird Sense*, describes an experiment carried out in the fifties on night-migrating robins. The birds followed their route unerringly, even when they couldn't see the stars. The suspicion arose that in some way they were sensitive to the magnetic poles of the earth. To confirm this Friedrich Merkel and Wolfgang Wiltschko changed the direction of the magnetic field with a powerful electromagnetic coil. The robins in the laboratory adjusted their position exactly as if they'd been using a compass. How birds sense the magnetic field is still not fully understood. It's generally accepted that some part is played by microscopic crystals of magnetite found around their nostrils.

The first rounds set out at dawn. The sun is clambering up the sleepy sky from the far shore of the lake. Getting up is like taking an icy cold shower. You have to do it without thinking, before the body can protest. In the early morning, everything in the tent is cold and damp from condensation. After a frosty night the flysheet is often stiff as parchment. At dawn there's usually the greatest number of birds; we spend so much time at the nets that after returning to camp we have to set out again immediately on the next rounds. Breakfast comes only after the second or third check. After that you eat constantly, every hour; a ringing camp is actually a festival of eating. Till evening, the time between rounds is filled with food and drink.

Sandwiches with luncheon meat (Tyrolean, English, Polish), jam sandwiches, pot noodles and lots of garlic. Ketchup. Junk food that I wouldn't touch at home, here tastes divine. Coffee and tea – particularly noteworthy is Minutka Tea, which has the savour of boiling water. And every hour there's a rapid march on either a long or a short round, depending on the conditions, in wellington boots or waders. Theoretically, after each contact with a bird we should wash our hands, but by day two few people remember to. In their distress, the birds often poo directly onto the hands that are disentangling them. The droppings are usually yellowish, but thrushes that have stuffed themselves with blueberries have purple excrement. Apparently, bacteriological analyses of the sacks used to transport the birds have sometimes revealed anthrax spores.

Participants say that little has changed in the camps since the sixties. Technological progress has inevitably left its mark: headlamps have appeared, allowing you to work with both hands, and the tents have zippers instead of ties. Also, a heating stove turned up in the canteen tent. For half a century it was believed that changes of temperature would lead to an epidemic of colds. Eventually someone brought a heater, and going back to the old pioneer days was out of the question. No one felt like sitting in damp clothing, warming hands and body over a candle flame on a November evening. Also, ethical standards have changed. Veterans knew the taste of long-tailed duck (good) and of the oystercatchers that run along the shore (bad). Prize specimens were killed and stuffed, for instance a stray American junco. Today such a killing, even in the interests of science, would be hard to imagine.

Humans like record holders – those who jump the furthest, run the fastest, lift the heaviest weights. They're excited by the most beautiful, the richest (are they the most resourceful?), or quite simply the most famous. This fascination extends to animals. On TV there's any number of nature thrillers with a perverse subtext: the most poisonous, the most dangerous, the ugliest. Why bother yourself with what's average?

Bird migration is for me the greatest miracle in nature. The story of each journey can be seen as a heroic odyssey. Every participant is exceptional. How many obstacles, discomforts, hardships and dangers does a tit weighing ten or fifteen grams encounter on its journey of a mere few hundred miles? Or the wallcreeper, that high-mountain eccentric with crimson wings. It migrates from its rocky crag down into the valleys, barely ten miles or so. Yet it's a journey between two realities: from the barren granite cliffs swept by the constant howling wind, to the peace and safety of spruce forests, and mountain villages with warmed concrete walls that even in winter are buzzing with insects.

But that's how we are: we remember those who stand tall on

the podium. How could we not admire the Arctic tern which, in its search for endless daytime, journeys from Greenland to Antarctica? Every year this greatest of bird wanderers travels 40,000 miles and is the most sun-exposed organism on the planet. When Greenland's summer ends, the Arctic tern heads south to the environs of the other pole. There, everything is coming to life after the polar winter. The Arctic tern traverses the Atlantic lengthwise, often crossing it as well – birds that follow the coastline of Europe sometimes cut across to South America and continue their journey there. A bird that lives thirty years (and there are such cases) thus has well over a million miles on its odometer. What does this hero look like? It's a smallish white-and-grey bird with a black cap, sharply pointed wings, and a heavenly long tail. Perhaps that's where its Latin epithet of *paradisaea* comes from?

The last daily round sets out in darkness, with only the light of LED lamps to guide us. Shifting shadows of branches, phosphorescent birch trunks, sudden gusts of wind, and leaves trembling on the trees. At times there's the thud of boars running in the night, or the splash of some heavy body plunging into the lake. Then silence, in which you can hear only the wind and your own breathing. Then, from time to time the fleeting shadow of a startled bird. On the dune a wren brushes me with its wing. It flies up like a large, dark-brown moth, perches on a low pine tree and watches, hypnotised by the light. I turn my headlamp off for a moment. After a second the dark, spherical form hops down into the lower branches.

I try not to think of the old apple trees near the campsite, the faint outlines of foundations, and the fact that, before the war, people lived and died here on our uninhabited spit. The night round stirs irrational thoughts. It's often disagreeable, it's true; but you can't just hurry past the nets. The lower parts have to be carefully checked, because that's where night-time stragglers get caught as they pass through the undergrowth. A brief glance isn't enough, the whole net must be examined. In reduced light the birds hanging there close to the ground bear an uncanny resemblance to fallen leaves. After dusk they pretty much stop fighting back; they're passive in their interrupted stupor. Blinded by the torchlight, they don't even try to slip from your fingers. It's dark in the birch wood; little light from the sky makes it through the small leaves. A bird suffering from stress, hanging in an unnatural position and sodden with dew, will quickly lose body heat, and in the morning will be no more than a limp bundle of feathers.

In the net on the dune, in a cloud of soft down I find the body of a blackbird. The life has gone from its half-open eye. Its head rocks inertly; its still-warm form slides easily out of the net. On its back are two small perforations from which a little blood has oozed. Blackbirds have weak hearts; this one was probably already dozing on a branch when something attacked it. In fact, most thrushes panic in the nets, flapping their wings, their bellies rubbing helplessly against the pockets of netting, leaving a trail of torn-out feathers. My night-time blackbird fled, got tangled up in the net, and evidently its heart gave out.

It's not just humans that are afraid in the night.

I marvel at godwits. These long-billed sea birds, which in flight resemble spindles, fly from their breeding grounds in Alaska to New Zealand. Seven thousand miles. And it's not just the distance, but the fact that the godwits cover it without a break, flying day and night for eight days. In other words, they cross the vast Pacific Ocean in a single stage. During the flight the godwits burn part of their digestive tract, and even some of the muscles keeping them in the air, for fuel. With each moment the bird is lighter, and thus the organism requires less and less power to move. The godwit is probably close to the limits of possibility as far as aerodynamic shape and energy management are concerned. Its nonstop journey has no equal, for one simple reason – there's no greater distance on earth that would have to be completed in a continuous flight.

No less impressive is the feat of hummingbirds, which weigh three grams. On their way to their wintering grounds in Cuba they cross the Mexican Gulf. Imagine this speck at the mercy of the Caribbean winds, which can so easily turn into hurricanes. How many grams make it to the destination? Can birds that weigh no more than a teaspoon of salt actually become a shadow of themselves? In fact, we have a comparable example in our own parts. Goldcrests, the smallest birds in Europe, cross the Baltic from Sweden. They often rest on the beach, exhausted, right under the feet of holidaymakers. It takes a little while for them to warm themselves in the sun and regain

A godwit mid-flight

their strength, then they set off into the pines along the shore in search of small insects.

Birds are capable of massive exertions at elevations where, for a human, every step is agony. Bar-headed geese regularly fly over the Himalayas; they've been spotted at altitudes approaching that of Mount Everest. Not far behind are stately whooper swans, which also live in Poland, and which are sometimes seen from aeroplanes. The record holder, though, is Rüppell's vulture, which has been observed at an unreachable 11,000 metres. Lapwings fly at almost 4,000 metres, while flocks of fieldfares, which in the autumn eat up the rowanberries and apples from abandoned orchards, migrate at just below that altitude.

The slender, elegant godwits dip their long bills in the sand up to their necks. No bird on this beach reaches so far. The waves chase a bright sanderling, which has found a few morsels on the temporarily exposed shoals. Shore birds' bills differ in length and shape. They're specialised pieces of equipment capable of sensing the slightest tremor underfoot. In the Vistula estuary the waders and seabirds (Charadriiformes) are ringed by the Kuling Water Bird Research Group. Here there are no nets, only tunnel traps. Set up on the ground, they look like large four-legged spiders with square bodies made of netting. Long arms, known as fences, lead from two entrances. The birds, feeding along the line of the surf, follow the fences straight into the netted chamber. Entering the trap is easy; exiting isn't.

Camp volunteers live in a beach cabin on the Mewia Łacha

Reserve. Even in August, at five in the morning the Baltic shore is freezing cold and hard as asphalt. A flock of curlews, with their long, melancholically curved beaks, flies over low and heads for the narrow mouth of the Vistula estuary. The first round involves laboriously pulling traps half-buried in seaborne sand out of the water. The birds have not yet begun feeding. Long, soft strands of seaweed have attached themselves to the metal frame. On the beach amid millions of broken shells are thousands of pieces of litter. Grilling forks with tines broken by the waves; bottles; dozens of plastic holders for toilet fresheners. (How ridiculously long-lived these objects are.) Sanitary towels bob like rays on the water, majestically waving their wings.

First there's a pinkish glow, then the orange sickle of the sun slowly emerges from beyond the horizon. In the mist, the boundary between water and sky has become blurred. In fact, here their close relation is plain. In the morning the sea is choppy, foaming into angry crests, while the white-streaked sky foretells surprises. In the afternoon the heated sand will burn your bare feet. Monster-sized cumulus clouds will bloom in the sky and surround the beach on all sides. Towards evening the terrifying dark-blue shadow of a thunderhead will crush the earth beneath its mass. A storm on a flat, treeless beach can be cataclysmic. No wonder lightning was an attribute of the most powerful deities.

When the time for migration comes around, birds stockpile energy. Their hormones increase their appetite. The sedge warbler, a small reed bird with a striped head, eats so compulsively that it doubles its mass, thanks to which it can cover 2,000 miles in a single uninterrupted flight. It usually takes three to four days. Actually, the amount of fat tells us a lot about a bird's condition. The ringer lays the bird on its back in his or her palm, takes the head between second and third fingers, and blows a steady stream of air on the region of the sternum. This place is called the furcula. Bare skin gleams beneath the feathers. The ringer assesses the amount of fat on the bird's belly on a scale from zero to eight. Zero and one augur poorly for surviving the migration.

Weather is a crucial factor for the traveller. Many birds get lost in fog; others, blown off course by a strong wind, end up in entirely unexpected places. Recovering from setbacks not only prolongs the journey, but also uses up reserves of energy. However, birds have ways of conserving their strength. Small inconspicuous hoods can lower body temperature at night so less energy is used. Western yellow wagtails and pipits, which fly across the desert, sit out the greatest heat in rock crevices. Birds react immediately to changes in the weather. In a head wind they fly low to the ground, sheltering behind rises in the terrain. In tail winds, they rise high up so as to take advantage of the helping hand.

The difficulties of their journey are shown in the 2001 film *Winged Migrations* by Jacques Perrin, a monumental tale of bird migrations. It's somewhere between nature documentary and feature film (there's a recurring hero – a goose with a piece of netting attached to its foot). An hour and a half, virtually without words – only music (our heart strings are tugged by the emotional blackmail of the strings) and the sounds of nature. The pale blue of polar ice, the rusty red of the American desert, the green of rice paddies, and the camera accompanying the migrating flocks. And also perils. Factory smoke, oil spills, traps set by hunters, and also violent storms that force the barnacle geese to rest on a battleship. The tern dragging a broken wing behind it doesn't stand a chance. Given the prospect of death by starvation, it's actually an act of mercy that it's set upon and eaten by crabs. Every year, up to eighty per cent of young swallows and half the adult birds from Great Britain perish during the migration season. Three quarters of young storks, raised with such great effort, fail to return to Poland in the spring. Natural selection is ruthless – only the strongest and the canniest survive.

I'm not a ringer. I don't analyse tables and columns filled with numbers, don't monitor migration routes, don't follow fluctuations in populations. I check the nets, extract the captured birds, chop wood, make dinner. I help the scientists. They're the ones who, in these times of climate change, transformations of the landscape and growing strain caused by humankind, must keep their fingers on the pulse. While I – I stare into the amber eye of a crested tit. I confirm at first hand that marsh warblers really do have exceptionally soft feathers, and that a coal tit smells of sap. I will never be closer to birds.

JAMES BOND & CO.

HE WAS BORN IN PHILADELPHIA in 1900, and throughout his life there was something of the nineteenth century about him. He was interested in nature from childhood. The prize butterfly specimens in his cabinets were probably brought back by his father, who led a scientific expedition to the Orinoco delta. His mother died the year the Great War broke out. The orphaned father and son moved to England, where the boy attended Harrow School and then Cambridge University. After his studies he returned to the United States and took a position in banking in his hometown. Yet he gave up his job a few years later in order to take part in an expedition to the lower Amazon. He served as a kind of secretary, writing descriptions of the species acquired. After returning home he grew interested in the avifauna of the Caribbean – the birds that lived on hundreds of tiny islands scattered across the ocean.

In 1963 he published his most important work, *Birds of the West Indies*, which is also known by the somewhat longer title of *Field Guide to the Birds of the West Indies: A Guide to All the Species of Birds Known from the Greater Antilles, Lesser Antilles and Bahama Islands*. He published widely in professional journals. He proved among other things that Caribbean birds descended from North American species. In recognition of his contributions he was awarded the Brewster Medal, the highest honour of the American Ornithologists' Union. He died in Philadelphia in 1989. His name was Bond. James Bond.

In his book *The Verb 'To Bird'*, Peter Cashwell, a teacher and linguist, describes a syndrome called BCD or Birding Compulsive Disorder. This complaint, an invention of the author, refers to the exclusive focus on birds specific to ornithologists. The syndrome is responsible for sudden braking in heavy traffic without checking the rear-view mirror when something of interest has flashed by at the side of the road. It also causes the birder to shush everyone in the middle of a conversation and raise a finger in the direction of an interesting sound.

'Birding is not a hobby, any more than sneezing is … or liking the color blue is. It is not something one chooses to do so much as something one cannot help but do,' Cashwell writes. He's a typical member of his class: at home he has a record collection and a sizeable library. He knows the famous writers and their works; he has no problem discussing East Asian philosophy or opera. But all that is set aside when some interesting specimen perches on the bird feeder. At such a moment, whatever the circumstances, every birder reaches for their binoculars.

For Cashwell, an example of a BCD attack is a series of thirty photographs of gulls he took on holiday, from a distance of 500 metres. He describes the sufferer in the style of neurologist and author Oliver Sacks: 'Inside his swiveling head is a normal human brain, with all the intelligence of a normal person, but tragically, he will never do normal things – read a book, drive to the store, or play outside with his children – without his head swinging around at the slightest perception of movement. Somewhere in his brain is a misfiring, a small electrical or chemical flaw, that will allow him no peace. He is caught forever in the prison that is BCD.'

Graduates of polytechnics, elementary schools, Slavic departments. Miners, trade reps and unemployed people. Rich folk festooned with £5,000 worth of Swarovski gear, and possessors of modest Soviet binoculars through which the world looks a little yellower. Birding is democratic. Its only real dividing line is between amateurs and scientists, though at times the capabilities of the one and the other are surprisingly complementary. The former are more impulsive. They're inclined to take an interest in the fate of every creature and to act in an imaginative way that is sometimes fuelled by blithe ignorance. The latter, on the other hand, see the big picture. Their professional training allows them to better understand the complex mechanisms that rule the world of nature.

I never thought seriously about becoming a professional ornithologist. I was afraid that studying biology would be boring and hard. In my family no one had a degree in the hard sciences, and in the end I followed the beaten path. My friend Witek, a physicist by training, told me a story that in his view speaks of a worrying if marginal aspect of professional biology. He read an article in a disciplinary journal about the frequency with which a certain wader would probe the ground. The researcher simply counted how often the bird stuck its bill in the mud at the water's edge as it fed. It's hard to think of a task like that with any enthusiasm.

The most interesting places for exchanges of ideas between professionals and amateurs are no doubt the online forums and mailing lists. Birders share their local sightings, and swap professional articles and titbits. An excellent example of BCD is my favourite story about a birdwatcher and the *Teleexpress* TV news programme. There was a piece about the musician Muniek Staszczyk, who was standing in his garden talking about something when a distinctive bird call was heard in the background. The birdwatcher, who was doing something in the next room, pricked up his ears. The sound was that of a greenish warbler. I don't know what Muniek was saying, no one on the forum was interested in that. The only thing that mattered was that little Siberian warbler, a rarity in the Warsaw region.

It's the same with films. There's a lot of discussion about audio tracks on which bird calls are heard that are not right for the time of year. Kraków in March, with heaps of melting snow, in Andrzej Wajda's *Katyń*, while over the rooftops we hear the chirping of swifts, which arrive in May. The song of the oriole, which leaves for Africa in August, can be heard in some autumn episodes of the Polish TV series *More Than Life At Stake*. A winter episode of another Polish series, the police procedural *Come In, 07*, apparently includes the springtime rasping of the corncrake. There are other curiosities too. The computer-generated vulture-ravens of Ridley Scott's *Kingdom of Heaven* make the sound of cranes. And then there's the stork with a ring on its leg in Wajda's *Pan Tadeusz*, over those early nineteenth-century 'fields adorned with many-coloured grain'.

Ian Fleming, former British intelligence agent, was vacationing at his villa in Jamaica. He'd long been intending to write a series of spy novels. As an avid birdwatcher he owned a copy of *Birds of the West Indies*. The moment his glance fell on the spine of the book, Fleming knew what his hero would be called. The first instalment of the adventures of James Bond, Her Majesty's secret agent with a licence to kill, became a bestseller. For several years the ornithologist from Philadelphia was unaware of the worldwide splash made by agent 007, who bore his name.

A few years after the novel *Casino Royale* came out, Mr Bond's wife wrote Fleming an indignant letter. How could he have used someone else's identity without permission? Especially that of a respected academic! Fleming must have felt sheepish, but he explained himself, if rather clumsily: 'It struck me that this brief, unromantic, Anglo-Saxon and yet very masculine name was just what I needed, and so a second James Bond was born.' He offered compensation: 'In return I can ... offer you or James Bond unlimited use of the name Ian Fleming for any purposes you may think fit. Perhaps one day your husband will discover a particularly horrible species of bird which he would like to christen in an insulting fashion by calling it Ian Fleming.'

Fleming also wrote to Bond himself. A somewhat belated request to make use of his name met with a brief, Bondlike response from the ornithologist: 'Very well.' The apology was accepted. Bond and his wife later visited the writer in his Jamaican house. In 1964 Fleming sent the ornithologist his latest 007 book – *You Only Live Twice* – with a dedication: 'To the real James Bond from the thief of his identity.' A few years later the copy was sold at auction for over $80,000.

Polish ornithological terminology has certain gaps. We haven't come up with effective translations of the words 'birdwatching' and 'birdwatcher', which allow the English to name an activity involving the non-professional observation of birds. There are many more of these amateurs than trained professionals. The Polish equivalents '*ptasiarstwo*' and '*ptasiarz*' are used in colloquial speech, but in formal contexts they seem rather childish. A '*ptakolub*' or 'bird-liker' sounds infantile, while 'ornitolog amator' can't been taken seriously, merely underlining the lack of qualifications. '*Obserwator ptaków*' or 'observer of birds' is little more than a synonym, while '*ornitolog*' itself is reserved for specialists. I don't feel comfortable using this term to refer to myself. It appears we're back where we started, and that '*ptasiarz*' will have to do.

Die Another Day was one of those low-grade, indistinguishable Bond films with Pierce Brosnan in the title role. It's not the Irish actor's fault – in my view he was a pretty good 007, a little after the style of Roger Moore. Suave, but with a sense of humour. The point is that in the early 2000s Bond films became cheap thrillers that were made as if cinema had remained where it was twenty years before. The improbable exploits of the hero were part of the series' conventions, but now the screenwriters overreached themselves. Even the title songs were worse and worse. Nor did the stories have much in common with Fleming's novels.

Die Another Day was released forty years after the first Bond film, and for that reason it turned out to contain countless references to its predecessors. I'd have no reason for mentioning the movie were it not for one thread. In chasing the North Korean agent Zao, Bond finds himself in Havana. In the office of Raoul, a sleeper agent and manager of a cigar factory, he looks over the books on a shelf. He picks out one and glances at the cover. We see that it is *Birds of the West Indies*. The author's name isn't shown. Bond borrows the book and a pair of binoculars from Raoul.

In the next scene he's scanning a rocky island on which the Korean is hiding. He wouldn't be himself, though, if he didn't also check out a beautiful woman emerging from the water (Halle Berry). It's a nod to the famous scene in the first Bond film, *Dr. No*, in which statuesque Ursula Andress rises from the waves like Botticelli's Venus. The girl, whom Bond subsequently meets, is called Jinx. She was born, appropriately enough, on Friday 13th. With a flirtatious wink, Bond explains that he's come to Cuba for a spot of birdwatching. Jinx, meanwhile, is a bird herself, though she may not know it. She bears the name of a nymph who cast a spell on Zeus and was turned into a bird by Hera in revenge. *Jynx torquilla* is the Latin name of the wryneck – the only woodpecker that doesn't peck wood. When alarmed, it hisses furiously and turns its head like a snake.

Alfred Hitchcock's *The Birds* is one of few films in which birds have been given a significant role. Alas, it isn't a very positive one. For the sake of authenticity, during one scene the crew threw live birds at lead actress Tippi Hedren. After a week, filming had to be interrupted so she could recuperate. From today's perspective the crows superimposed onto the frame with the human actors look comical more than anything else. The same goes for the stuffed specimens attached to the clothing of those fleeing. All the same, the image of the swirling flock, of this irrational element, is highly suggestive. It's recorded somewhere in the subconscious, and no one who has seen *The Birds* can watch a dismal, croaking maelstrom of jackdaws and rooks and remain unaffected. Nor the flocks of starlings, many thousand strong, that gather at dusk and fill the evening air with their chattering disquiet.

In *The Birds* the aggressors are not birds of prey, killing machines with razor-sharp talons. The menace has a terrifyingly familiar and innocent face. In Hitchcock's film people are set upon by birds of the kinds that live in close proximity to us – gulls, crows, sparrows, starlings. It's true that in port towns gulls can get up to all kinds of mischief. I remember how on Brighton Pier they would snatch the food from people's plates. They were huge and brash; their yellow beaks with the red spot demanded respect, and few dared to protest. The holidaymakers

The wryneck woodpecker

would stuff down what was left, hoping to finish it before the gulls came back.

Hitchcock's birds act unnaturally. In one scene, some crows gather silently in front of a school. Anyone who has seen a flock of crows (or other corvids) even once knows that they're pretty noisy. Here, they're clearly up to something (with their collective intelligence). When the children emerge from the school the flock descends on them, screeching. The crows' ally is a shrewish, annoyingly know-it-all female ornithologist. She asserts that birds 'bring beauty to the world', and talks irrelevantly about the annual count. Everything in her appearance screams: eccentric old biddy.

The viewer increasingly wants her to get her comeuppance. And indeed, soon the gulls attack, as if complying with that desire. They cause a fire in the centre of town. The ornithologist is crushed – her idealistic vision of the world is shattered.

The Slovenian philosopher Slavoj Žižek explains *The Birds* using Freud: the creatures' aggression as a product of the sexual tension between the three main characters. Is the flock bursting out of the chimney an explosion of incestuous energy on the part of the mother, who refuses to share her son with his fiancée? I couldn't say. In my own superficial interpretation I focus on the figure of the ornithologist. Hitchcock takes the side of those who question authority and who are irked by the pontifications of experts – because not everything can be explained. 'Why are they doing it?' We don't know and we never will. The film instils in us a feeling that reality can rebel against us. Too bad Hitchcock chose birds to illustrate his thesis.

In 2005 Jonathan Franzen, a leading American writer, published an essay about how he got into birding. Its title is 'My Bird Problem', as if, as for Cashwell, it's once again a question of a sickness or an addiction. I've never read anything that so accurately captures the feelings of a person in the throes of this particular passion. The essay begins with a description of the South American masked duck. The author catches sight of the bird only briefly, after which it disappears in the reeds. On the way back to his car Franzen encounters some birders who, excited by his discovery, ask for details and write down his name. At the headquarters of the reserve he records the location of his sighting in a special notebook.

Then come agonies of doubt. Was it really a masked duck, or just a mirage, a dream of a rare species never seen before? Maybe the harsh afternoon light made the colour on the duck's cheeks look brighter, and a more common ruddy duck became a masked duck? The females of both species are very similar. Franzen isn't even worried about the problem of correct identification so much as his reputation. If no one else confirms his sighting, it'll look as if this Franzen guy doesn't know what he's talking about. He's afraid of loss of face.

No one else confirms the presence of the duck, and Franzen commits a series of mistakes over the following days of the trip: he confuses a green-winged teal with a wigeon; he quickly and wrongly identifies a peregrine falcon (which in reality is an osprey). The goal of infallible identification is an obsession with any ambitious birder. The less experienced ones tend towards premature determinations; old hands are more circumspect in their verdicts. I've lost count of the number of times I've been in too much of a hurry to identify a bird.

One spring morning J. and I were walking in the meadows along the Pilica River. All of a sudden, a brown bird burst out from under our feet with a flash of white tail feathers. 'Great snipe,' I said with total conviction, though its presence in those parts would have been a minor sensation. My companion stared in bafflement at the photograph he'd taken. I wouldn't even hear of doubts. All the same, J. lightened and cropped the photo and sent it out on the mailing list, where smarter colleagues congratulated him on his sighting of a mallard. How could I have been so wrong?

Franzen wouldn't be the great writer he is, though, if all he wrote about was the identification of birds. In 'My Bird Problem' he tells of a crisis in his marriage and about starting over. He talks about his quest for a life philosophy and about understanding nature. He admits that birdwatching was for him an escape from his everyday problems. But he would only do it from time to time. It wasn't until some friends showed him a veery in a city park that he fell into birding up to his ears. Why it was this plain little thrush that moved him so, I have no idea.

Franzen got interested in birds relatively late in life, even though he'd gone to school with the daughter of Phoebe Snetsinger, a legend of American ornithology. When in 1981 she was diagnosed with melanoma, she decided to spend the remaining months of her life birdwatching. She didn't have to worry about money because she was the daughter of advertising magnate Leo Burnett. Snetsinger ended up living for another twenty years; she interrupted her journeys around the world only when the illness returned and she needed a new course of chemotherapy. In the end, death, which had been hanging over her for many years, took her entirely unexpectedly. She died in Madagascar in a road accident. She had just seen a red-shouldered vanga when the driver of the car she was in fell asleep and the vehicle overturned. Her bird count stopped at what was then a record 8,450 species.

During one of his birding escapades, Franzen had the following thought: 'The well-adjusted throngs of collaborator birds in South Florida, both the trash pigeons and trash grackles and the more stately but equally tame pelicans and cormorants, all struck me now as traitors. It was this motley band of modest peeps and plovers on the beach who reminded me of the human beings I loved best – the ones who didn't fit in ... I'd been told that it was bad to anthropomorphize, but I could no longer remember why.'

Plovers – small, timid birds – like all waders avoid humans and adapt poorly to changes in the environment. They're incapable of exploiting the waste of civilisation, unlike the aforementioned 'traitors'. A similar philosophy is practised by Walter, the hero of Franzen's best-known book *Freedom*: 'The love he felt for the creatures whose habitat he was protecting was founded on projection: on identification with their own wish to be left alone by noisy human beings.' Many birdwatchers will find something worryingly familiar in Walter's misanthropy.

A seemingly placid interest in birds can at times turn into a contest. Birders and ornithologists keep lists of their accomplishments: life lists, year lists, regional lists. Birdwatching at times resembles a sport; the list can begin to rule the daily life of the birders. It makes them stand on a dune in a stinging sand storm, or wade out up to the waist in a freezing springtime bog. News of a rare bird showing up at the other end of the country can lead to a family vacation being broken off. Luckily not everyone yields to such pressures, not everyone is competitive. I know amateurs and professionals who have never seen relatively common species – spotting them was not important to them, or did not fall within their scientific interests.

I'm regularly asked who checks the lists. The answer is: no one, because it's all based on trust. Those who ask are usually surprised: 'But that means people can cheat!' Sure they can; but why would they? An impressive list is not associated with any measurable prestige. You're not going to get an advertising contract, Cashwell jokes. It's more a matter of fulfilling an ambition than seeking to impress someone else. Why deceive yourself? There are of course frauds, but their motivations are beyond me. Besides, not everything can be made up – sightings of birds that are found only infrequently in Poland are subject to verification by the Ornithological Section of the Fauna Committee of the Polish Zoological Society. In the case of very rare species photographic or sound documentation is required. Small-time duplicity would become a big lie. A mishap of that sort leads to ostracism from the community.

The film *Kes*, directed by Ken Loach, portrays the mining town of Barnsley and its inhabitants. Most of the actors were amateurs whose accents were so thick that for American viewers the audio track had to be re-recorded. The effect of profound realism was further enhanced by the use of natural light for the cinematography. The world of Barnsley is a dismal one in this rendering; the story itself is hardly more cheerful. Billy Casper is a teenage outsider growing up in desperate poverty. His family home is so small that the boy has to share a bed with his older brother Jud, who gets up every day at dawn to go to work at the mine. Such a job is the most Billy can hope for in the future.

The boy wanders aimlessly around the town; he has a paper round; he gets into trouble at school. It doesn't look as though he'll amount to much. But one day, as he's walking through a wood on the outskirts of town, he sees a kestrel hunting. He watches fascinated as the bird hovers, slices through the air in agile twists, then perches on an old stone wall. Billy shoplifts a book on falconry from a second-hand bookshop, and one day takes a grown chick from the nest. It's a female; the boy names it Kes. Every day he procures some meat for it and tries to school it, though he says that a kestrel can't be trained – at most it can be taught to cooperate. Or perhaps the bird is taming the boy?

Billy lets himself be carried away by a fantasy. He wants to be like a kestrel, free, unconstrained, independent; yet the institutions of the state, and his strict teachers at school, have him down for a job at the mine. This sensitive dreamer from the lower depths cannot count on any other destiny. His kestrel, raised from a chick, is also far from free; it doesn't know liberty and doesn't need it. Wild birds only seem to be free. True, they're not bounded by space. But their flight has to have some goal. They're driven by instinct, not by fancy. They won't abandon their offspring on a whim, and their autumn and spring migrations are not pleasure trips but a struggle for life. Stories like *Kes* never end well, especially when they're intended to make us angry at the injustice of the world. The kestrel is killed by the brutish Jud to punish his little brother for the theft of a small sum. The death of the bird means the end of his illusions. All that remains is drab reality, covered in the soot of the mine.

I find similarities between the tale of *Kes* and the movie *Birdman of Alcatraz*, which, incidentally, is based on a true story. The imposing Burt Lancaster plays Robert Stroud, a lifer who has spent forty-three years in solitary confinement. This patent psychopath suddenly softens when on his daily walk in the prison yard he finds a sparrow chick blown from its nest by a strong wind. He's given permission by the prison authorities to keep the bird in his cell, and looks after it with great care. Here a comical element enters this bleak film. The precedent causes an avalanche: warbling canaries appear in the cells of every murderer, rapist and degenerate. But the other prisoners' zeal soon runs out, and one by one the birds end up with Stroud.

From Feto Gomez (Telly Savalas) Stroud acquires a female canary. He decides to breed birds in his cell. 'New life? In prison?' the guard says in astonishment. 'I guess it makes no difference to them. Canaries live in cages anyway,' replies the old-timer, who has no illusions. Only humans yearn for liberation when they're imprisoned. Let out of their cages, the birds flutter helplessly around the cell. They don't know what it means to be free. *Birdman of Alcatraz* is about successful resocialisation and the ruthlessness of the system. Stroud, though he barely has a third-grade education, reads academic textbooks and scientific studies. He comes up with medications for common ailments of domesticated birds. The results of his research are published in professional journals, and universities offer him grants. But he never leaves the prison. Perhaps it's better to be a canary, and not know the taste of freedom.

Just as with 'birdwatcher', the Polish language is helpless when faced with the term 'twitcher' – no decent Polish equivalent has surfaced. We talk and write about 'Tłiczowanie' in reference to a particular kind of birding that mostly involves running around after rare species. Twitch, of course, in English means a nervous tic. A twitcher is a jumpy person. Twitchers are capable of travelling hundreds of miles to see (or 'tick') a new species. The location is announced by other birdwatchers, and so in this sense twitching is a kind of parasitism. But you have to be quick about it – the bird might fly away at any moment, or be scared off by birders who got there before you.

Stereotypical twitchers barely glance at the bird; they tick the species off on their list and go back to waiting for the next sensation. They monitor forums and sites offering information about rarities, and receive text messages about significant sightings. Twitching is not widely respected in the birding community, because it doesn't bring any particular benefit. Indeed, at times it can be harmful, when birds are disturbed and have to move elsewhere. A person can speak with pride of a bird they themselves have discovered. To call someone a twitcher is really a kind of insult – one that surfaces from time to time in online slanging matches.

This somewhat degraded form of birdwatching originated of course in birding-mad Britain. When a rare bird appears in someone's garden, mayhem ensures: thousands of twitchers descend on the neighbourhood, to the point that the police have to close off the surrounding streets. Six million inhabitants of the British Isles watch birds; they form a keen-eyed network, and so interesting species are seen there relatively frequently. Furthermore, birds from North America are regularly blown onto the Isles, and there are also often rare species from Siberia. Among fanatical birders fights occasionally break out; people have been known to faint, even have heart attacks. Every year devotees spend tens of thousands of pounds travelling around the country.

I'm not without fault myself – I've twitched a bird or two, though I try to put rational limits on my madness. For instance, I don't twitch species that don't especially interest me, nor those for which I'd have to travel halfway across the country. I wasn't prepared to go all the way to Racibórz in the south-west to see an American lesser yellowlegs. It looks a little like our common greenshank – somehow not exotic enough to get so very excited about. But if it had landed on Zegrzyński Inlet, an hour from home, that would have been a different matter entirely. Visitors from the far north – two-barred crossbills – I twitched week after week. The second trip, to the outskirts of the town of Mława, was successful. The lovely, bright red birds were shelling seeds from larch cones. Their strange, crooked bills are perfectly adapted for the task. The upper and lower mandibles cross at the tip, creating a kind of pincers. At one time it was believed that the crossbill had tried to extract the nails from Christ's body, and in this way had twisted its bill.

It was early afternoon, the sun was reflecting furiously off the snow, and we were passing one another on the Długa Łuka boardwalk in the Biebrza Marshes. Usually the manoeuvre is a simple one, since the path is pretty wide, but this time it was covered with snow. One incautious step off the narrow beaten track and you could end up in the marsh. The Polish politician Janusz Palikot was coming in the opposite direction, a decent pair of binoculars round his neck – Leica or Swarovsky – I didn't get a good look. He returned my 'good afternoon' and raised the binoculars to his eyes. A flock of white-fronted geese flew overhead. I regarded him more favourably after that.

Another politician, Włodzimierz 'Baron' Czarzasty, once said that he devotes 'at least a month each year' to his passion for ornithology. He even boasted: 'I just came back from the Narew and Biebrza Valley, where I was observing ruffs.' Golden-tongued and witty as ever, he likened fellow politician Donald Tusk to a harpy eagle. He explained: 'It's a bird of prey, like a regular eagle or a buzzard, but it's more vengeful. It hunts in the woods by evening'. The vision of the then prime minister chasing after monkeys through the treetops and crushing their skulls in his powerful talons somehow stayed with me. Yet harpy eagles are no more vengeful than say, rooks are embittered. What will people not do for a striking comparison.

Still speaking of our politicians, somewhere on some disk I have a photograph showing Jarosław Kaczyński sitting on a bench in the parliament chamber studying a book. It can't have been an important vote, since next to him Mariusz Błaszczak is talking on his mobile phone. Maybe it's a break in proceedings? Whatever. The point is that Kaczyński is reading about one of the rarest of the Polish birds of prey, the greater spotted eagle. He's examining the dark form of an adult bird and a brightly speckled juvenile. When I look at the photo, I think to myself: he can't be a bad man. Does he meet in secret with his political enemies Palikot and Czarzasty to pursue the hobby they have in common?

Ornithologists in movies are rarely strong, determined men of action, but there are exceptions. For instance there is Raymond Tusk in the US version of *House of Cards*, a businessman and energy magnate. The main hero of the series, the ruthless, cynical politician Frank Underwood, is to visit him at his home and offer him the position of vice-president. Frank is tormented by envy, since he believes the job is rightfully his; he doesn't know that this is merely a test. In reality he's the one under consideration for the vice-presidency, while Raymond's job is to vet Underwood.

Frank, then, is filled with resentment, while Tusk is enjoying himself immensely. He takes the other man down into his garden and points out some woodpecker to him. He's an amateur orni-thologist, which is to say, a classic eccentric. Frank looks directly at the viewer (this being one of the series' trademarks) in disdain and mockery. 'What a bore,' his expression says. Birdwatching is a frivolous occupation, when they ought to be speaking about the one thing that interests Underwood – power. We of course agree with him: from the beginning we've been hostages and mute accomplices to his villainy. Yet Tusk thumbs his nose at him and upsets his plans. Frank in turn begins by treating him with scorn, then sees his true worth, and finally destroys him. Just as he destroys every obstacle in his way.

The compulsion to watch birds is the basis for the American comedy film *The Big Year*, directed by David Frankel. Despite the star-studded cast, the film was a gigantic flop at the box office. The reviewers weren't excessively positive either, which is hardly surprising – the movie at most raises a weak smile. What is the 'big year' of the title? An uninterrupted twelve-month twitching marathon of bird species within the United States, from Attu Island in Alaska, via the Nevada desert, to the mangrove forests of Florida. Many birders take a year off work for this purpose. The record holder has the renown of an Olympic medallist within the community.

The three heroes have to contend not only with their rivals but also with their own problems. Stu Preissler (Steve Martin) is the CEO of a large company who's about to retire; he's afraid of not having anything to do, and is wrestling with the temptation to return to work. Brad Harris (Jack Black) is the classic loser. A divorcé in the throes of a midlife crisis, he lives with his parents and has to ask for financial help with his birding from his father, who disapproves of his son's hobby. The current record holder is Kenny Bostick (Owen Wilson), whose bird-watching obsession has already led to one divorce. As we watch, he destroys another marriage in his quest for victory.

The film makes no attempt to explain why people are willing to take part in this gruelling competition with no prizes. It's a summer family movie. The race, and its unwritten rules, seem nonsensical to people who barely notice the existence of birds. *The Big Year* seems to aim to convince people that ornithology is not boring and birdwatchers aren't mad, but all it does is confirm stereotypes. The reviewer in *The Daily Telegraph* hit the nail on the head: films about eccentrics require an eccentric approach. Maybe if the movie had been directed by Wes Anderson?

In Poland, including sightings from 1801 to 1950, over 450 bird species have been recorded. Some of them appeared only once. A birder usually begins with a life list. At some point the game becomes a little frustrating, because new species are added to the list less and less frequently, unless you shift into high gear and chase around after every rarity. After 300 species the emotions begin to cool. What can be done to keep the fire burning? Begin a year list. Or the increasingly popular Western Palearctic list. This is the part of our biogeographic realm (the Palearctic) that stretches from the Urals and the Caucasus to the Azores and from Spitsbergen to North Africa (including the Arabian peninsula). We're evidently able to afford long-distance travel these days.

To assemble a decent year list, a birder from the Mazowsze

region begins by scanning the fields around Warsaw. Sometimes small flocks of Arctic passerines stray this way, while the rough-legged buzzard, our northern bird of prey, is watching over things. When the frosts get stronger, it's worth popping up to the Baltic – at such times sea birds come closer to the shore. Early spring is the time of courtship rituals of owls and woodpeckers. Geese will soon be on the move too. Flocks of many thousands in V-formation have taken a fancy to certain fields in the Łódź region. In April and May you can take trips to the Biebrza Marshes. The lekking of ruff and great snipe, moose pensively munching on fresh shoots – all this can be found less than 120 miles from the capital. At the end of May and beginning of June it has to be the Tatra Mountains.

Then comes the most dismal time of year for the birder: summer. The woods fall silent, in the sky there's only the tireless skylark, the yellowhammer chirps in the heat. Birds and their offspring hide deep among the leaves. But by the beginning of August the autumn migration begins. First to set off are warmth-loving birds, so it's worth a visit to the uncultivated fields of the Lublin area. Stately short-toed eagles soar there, while nimble red-footed falcons chase around after insects close to the heated earth. Flocks of plovers also fly over Poland after leaving their breeding grounds in the north. Autumn is one vast extended migration. It's good to watch it by the sea: many migrating birds follow the coastline. October and even November are the months for geese and cranes. The largest congregations are to be found in the estuary of the Warta and in the Barycz Valley. Then silence falls again, as the bird year draws to a close.

HARBOTKA

AN OLD COTTAGE, RELOCATED FROM the Kurpie region, with traces of blue paint on a dangling shutter. The place has been eaten away by bark beetle, to the point that every spring I'm surprised it's still standing. There are old friends too. A woodpecker, which often used to wake me by hammering on the shutter, and which has for many years availed itself of this mouldering pantry. It also often visits a birch grove that soughs deafeningly on stormy days, as its supple trunks sway in the wind. I hang my hammock there, and the birds quickly grow accustomed to its red colour – the song thrush almost fell into it once during a crazy pursuit of a butterfly. Close by the birches, aspens tremble in their timorous way. They quake even when there's no wind. Only the old oaks are silent: they won't yield to just any breeze.

A mouse in the undergrowth near the door drags a twist of spaghetti behind it. In the daytime it has nothing to fear – foxes disappeared from Harbotka ten or fifteen years ago. Leaves cover up dozens of entrances to old burrows, and the unused tunnels have collapsed for good. But at dusk the mouse cannot feel safe, because black-eyed tawny owls take over the neighbourhood. A ruddy-coloured one and a grey one. They can't live without one another. When they're not hunting together, they call to each other and wait for a response. They probably live in an old hole left by a black woodpecker. Yesterday, after a gap of many years, I heard its protracted call again.

The blackcap by the rotting outhouse seems unable to come to terms with having to share its territory with a human. 'Tset, tset, tset'; it raises the black feathers on its head and looks at me indignantly. It's the same with the blackbird – it flies off with a cry whenever I go among the blackthorn. It's a panic-monger, but I respect it – I've seen it sneaking past me to feed its young. It's constantly at work; barely has it arrived with a caterpillar in its beak before it's rushing off for another. And not half-heartedly or reluctantly, but at full speed, as if it were being chased by something. It's in a hurry; after all, this is a second, late brood. Before long the evenings will start to get cold.

From time to time the sparrowhawk, that little demon of death, comes by too. It's especially fond of that dry branch over the roof. It perches and looks around for a while with its keen, darting eye. It makes decisions at lightning speed; its life clearly operates at a faster pace than ours. It drops abruptly into the orchard. Murderously speedy and agile, it dodges between the branches. I see it reach out its long talons rapaciously, trying to snatch the serins and goldfinches that are scattering. This time it has missed; it flies off nonchalantly towards the river. Maybe it'll catch some unsuspecting little bird down there?

Why 'Harbotka'? Apparently the squire liked to admire the view of the river valley over tea, or 'herbata'. Maybe these old oaks remember him – the ones behind the house that I've climbed hundred of times, and that every autumn bombard the roof with their acorns? Maybe the pinewood cross to the unknown soldier from the First World War does? The locals say Harbotka is haunted. They come here to pick mushrooms, but they wouldn't visit by night, not on your life.

I understand the squire. From the top of the slope, stretching all the way to the horizon is a mosaic of meadows and of woods that are all that remains of the primeval forest. To the south is the church spire in Stromiec, to the west the chimneys of the power plant at Kozienice (those, the squire never even imagined). From the alders along the river, cranes are calling in the evening silence. They probably live on the far bank, beyond the place where the ferry and the ferryman's cottage used to be: an MZ motorcycle leaning against the wall, a room from a Van Gogh painting – chair and table.

The river can be reached by going down through the orchard. At the foot of the slope are the meadows where we used to gather flowers for the Feast of the Assumption. The road that the tractors use has been reinforced with a repurposed fibre cement roof – yes, it's toxic, but at least it won't harm whoever took it off their own roof. (And besides, it'd be a pity for it to go to waste.) Stands of alders. To the right, for a few years there was a chokeberry plantation, a passing fad.

A fork in the road. The way to the left leads down to the bridge, along the river that can barely be seen behind a line of willow trees. Right next to it is the wildest stretch of water. Close to the bank there are extensive shallows. One time, my father and I walked several hundred metres upstream. In my memory it was the upper reaches of the Amazon. Tangled lianas of hop, impenetrable thickets, overgrown islands untouched by human feet. I was excited to see the beautiful common reed buntings with their black heads – they used to be called 'reed sparrows' in Polish. I rattled on and on about the buntings, then that evening I went down with a fever and was ill for a week. 'The curse of the bunting,' my father said with assurance.

Usually, though, we go to the right, along the bank of the overgrown former river bed, alongside the meadow – which after our trip to Hungary we started calling, somewhat grandiosely, the *puszta*, in reference to the Hungarian plains. When I was a child it seemed boundless, especially in the faded colours of late summer. Someone put up goalposts, but I never saw anyone playing soccer there. The *puszta* had once been a pasture. Now there wasn't a single cow left in the village.

The *puszta* has changed. Ten or fifteen years ago, every spring, till June there was a lake here when the river flooded. I remember hundreds of birds – the silvery wings of terns glinting over the surface. When the waters dropped and the river unhurriedly resumed its usual course, satisfied with its annual demonstration of force, in the meadow there would be black-tailed godwits with their long bills and ruddy plumage, and nervous lapwings. At the slightest cause the latter would rise into flight on their wide, rounded wings. Most of all I like their call – tearful and plaintive, like the sounds when you turned the dials on an old transistor radio.

The water would remain only in the oozy, duckweed-covered old river bed. Carrying my clothes over my head, I'd wade through the bog in quest of skittish and elusive wood

A common reed bunting

sandpipers, which in summer liked to dabble in the sticky mud near the bank. There was also a colony of black terns, dogged and fearless when an intruder drew near to their nests. With their grating cries, they would swoop right over the heads of passing humans and animals. Much calmer was the vigilant marsh harrier that flew slowly over the grass in search of mice or birds' nests.

When the water rose high, the river current was dark and forbidding. At the bends, in the little trash-littered bays you would find objects brought from upstream: old refrigerators, toilet lids and long johns hanging in the low branches. Over time the clothing faded and dulled, and from a distance I sometimes mistook it for a heron standing in wait for small fish.

In the summer the current was usually tranquil, lazy, and yellowish from the sand at the bottom. In the course of time the beach grew bigger, plovers skittering over it like wind-up toys. Sokołowski writes that each one 'takes nine steps per second'. Just above the surface of the water a kingfisher would whizz by in a flash of emerald green. Its Polish name is '*zimorodek*' or 'winter-born', but it came into the world not in the wintertime but in the earth. Specifically, in a sandy bank on the far side of the river. People would drive down from the village in tractors with trailers and would take away a part of the beach. No landowner had laid claim to the river sand. And in such a way the beach finally ceased to exist.

The former river bed has grown over with water plants; today you'd look in vain for lapwings along its banks. The meadow is cropped not by gentle cows but by unfeeling mowers. Under their blades, and in the jaws of foxes inoculated against rabies, hundreds of small birds die every year. In the evening, when large-eyed deer bed down for the night amid the sweet flag, you can hear something that sounds a bit like the oink of a pig, perhaps the strangest sound in Polish nature: the diminutive water rail, secretive inhabitant of marshes, is announcing its presence before the night.

At dusk the sky clears; colours and shades melt away. The pink glow slowly fades. In the darkness the little yellow lamps of irises continue to glow. A clammy mist drifts close to the ground. By the light of the camera flash the structure of this cloud, with its whirling atoms of water vapour, is revealed. Near the wood there's a hurried crashing sound, the crack of branches, then the bleat of a young fawn. It's strange how closely it resembles the noises made by drunken soccer fans.

The cacophony of birdsong quietens, the creak of the great reed warbler subsides. The indefatigable nightingale remains at its post, while the corncrake adds its 'drap-drap-drap'. From the sedge comes the metallic reel of the river warbler, which sounds more like an insect than a bird. And it will stay this way till morning: nightingale, corncrake, river warbler, with a single anaemic laugh from the little crake.

Before four o'clock it's already light, but the milky haze reduces visibility to thirty metres. The repeated tune of the song thrush comes to life. The yellowhammer warms up with a broken-off phrase before it begins its all-day singing. The river warbler pauses its monotonous drumbeat, but only to change position on its branch. The corncrake approaches very close, and along with the drap-drap there's a strange echoing hum, as if its voice were being played back on a recording. I can see, not the bird itself, but its darting movements, marked only by shifts in the grasses bending under the weight of the dew. I hear the plash of long-fingered feet on the sodden meadow.

When alarmed, the corncrake prefers to flee on foot rather than rising into flight. I once held in my hand a water rail, its close cousin, and I was struck by how disproportionately strong and muscled its legs were. When the bird regained its freedom, it ran several dozen metres at a sprinter's dash before it took off. As it ran it looked for all the world like a chicken (which also has very strong legs, as it happens).

In the meantime, the unseen corncrake is circling round me, and for sure peeking at me from its hiding place in the grass. Its voice can rise to more than a hundred decibels; I feel my eardrums tauten from the strain. Finally, a few metres away, for a split second I see a drab-coloured head with a short bill that pokes out of the undergrowth then vanishes again at once. A moment later, 'drap-drap' resounds, fifty metres away already. I know I can't count on any more. I pull back and, standing by the wood, I watch the no-longer-threatened bird fly low over the meadow, its big legs dangling inertly. Its short tail prevents it from being able to brake normally, so it slows like a skier, turning at right angles to its flight path, and drops clumsily into the grass.

It's almost five, and the river warbler is gradually swallowed up amid the hullabaloo of hundreds of birds. I trudge through the grass that's wet as a dog's coat; within seconds my trousers are clinging tightly to my legs. In the mist it's hard to judge distance; sound travels somehow differently across the meadow. I pause every ten metres or so; the river warbler seems to be right there. But nothing comes of it. It's perched on a dry branch several dozen metres further away than I had thought. It sings frenziedly, as if the entire world around it did not exist – head tipped back, throat wide open, it quivers, resonating with its monotonous metallic song.

A July evening and I'm not going south towards the river, but northwards, among the squat rows of twisted apple trees that stretch all the way to the town of Grójec. In a month their boughs will be groaning under the weight of ripe fruit. The wild cherries are finished; the sour cherries darken in the sun. For the past month, the orchards have been rocked by the thunder of gas cannons – the eternal civil war between humans and untold hosts of starlings. The birds don't seem to be much bothered. The explosions only frighten my dog. Serins and goldfinches hop about on the stave of the telegraph wires.

Low down, just over the treetops, a female marsh harrier flies over. The smaller birds scatter noisily. Bright plumage on its head contrasts with its dark wings. Some people call it a 'blondie'. Its gaze meets mine for a moment and I see those ruthless, yellow, hypnotic eyes of a predator. The harrier family is neither the fastest nor the most lethal of the birds of prey, but for me they're the handsomest. And the most magnificent of all is Montagu's harrier, which alas is another victim of mechanised farming. Its nests and young are cut down along with the grain.

Montagu's harrier is elegance to a T – long, narrow wings and a shapely, not over-muscular body, with a broad head a little like an owl's. It's not the best build for rising in heated air; the limited wing surface prevents it from being able to soar amid the clouds, while a strong wind blows it in all directions. Nor do the narrow wings resemble the sickle-shaped curves of the falcon, which render its body superbly aerodynamic in an attack. A Montagu's harrier's wings serve for a stately patrol flight low over the meadows. I once observed a splendid light-grey male flying very slowly about a metre from the tips of the grasses. From a distance it looked as if he was almost motionless but, when the opportunity arose, he folded his wings in an instant, dived, and snatched up his victim.

The marsh harrier hunts in a similar way, but its natural hunting grounds are reed beds. 'Blondie' isn't fussy; it won't say no to a mouse, or to fieldfare chicks from the orchard. The dark bird shifts course; my presence could get in the way of its hunting. The orchard ends at a row of pine trees, on the far side of which I hear the descending trill of a woodlark. There isn't a more melancholy singer among Polish birds. It even owes its Latin name *Lullula* to its plaintive voice. It's a strange contrast to the vibrant, euphoric song of its close relative the skylark.

I pass along the trees, and all at once its song rings out directly above my head. The woodlark is flapping its wings lightly, virtually hanging in the air, and singing its accelerating melody into the evening stillness. I lie down on the short grass, which stinks of chemicals. These days the fruit trees are sprayed almost daily; Mendeleev is the patron saint of orchard owners.

Yet not all life can be poisoned away. I watch the woodlark for a few minutes, then it suddenly glides out of sight.

It's dark by the time I head home and I realise my phone isn't in my pocket. Maybe I left it on the table, I think, trying to fool myself. In my heart of hearts, though, I know it's there, in the orchard, beneath the woodlark that was overhead. And thus the evening has an unintended epilogue: I drive back among the rows of fruit trees. On the dirt track a big tractor politely lets me pass. I barely notice its underage driver with the mien of an old hand of forty. With my headlights I startle a fleeing young hare, whose eye shines like a tiny golden disk in the darkness. I wind my window down, but I can no longer hear the mournful tones of the woodlark, only the rumble of the tractor and the hiss of the nozzles. The mechanical monster moves through the orchard, its triple eye gleaming. I stop, take three steps to the left and, amazed at my own accuracy, pick a silver object from the ground. The wet screen reads 21:47.

THE BASILISK
IN THE FRYING PAN

3 January

IT TURNS OUT THAT A cluster of bushes is all that's needed to attract interesting birds. In the thickets above the so-called frying pan (the square in front of the Centrum metro station in Warsaw), every year the warbling of a nightingale can be heard. The place is basically used as a rubbish tip by itinerant sellers and as a toilet for the homeless, but the singer returns undeterred each night to intone its lament to the city's inhabitants. This tangle of vegetation also draws other, entirely unexpected birds. In the spring the song of the ortolan bunting has been heard here, as well as the improvisations of the marsh warbler and the screech of a great reed warbler. For the past month a barred warbler has been there. It's the first attempt by that species to winter in Poland. This individual has taken a particular liking to a barberry bush by the kilometre marker; its yellow eyes shine with a basilisk-like stare from the branches. The bird is not timid, and lets itself be photographed from a few metres away.

5 January

The spectre of 'revitalisation' has been hanging for some time over Skaryszewski Park, one of the oldest parks in the capital.

This word, fashionable in bureaucratic jargon, freezes the blood in the veins of lovers of urban greenery. Revitalisation, which according to its etymology should involve bringing something back to life, usually means cutting down bushes and trees. For the authorities, the ideal is sterile patches of grass trimmed as short as golf greens, and conifers that don't drop troublesome leaves – as on the computer visualisations of new neighbourhoods. A striking example of authorised vandalism was the revitalisation of the Krasiński Gardens. The original 'viewing axis' was restored. Bushes and several hundred trees were removed, including some that had survived the destruction of the city during the uprising of 1944. A view opened up onto Więźniów Politycznych Stalinizmu Square ('Political Prisoners of Stalinism Square'), and the high wall of the Chinese Embassy. The number of bird species dropped by 50 per cent.

In Skaryszewski Park they're also threatening to recreate the layout from 100 years ago. Avenues of old lindens and ash trees are in danger. Once again it's a question of whether urban green spaces are supposed to be no more than an aesthetically pleasing front that looks good on the plans. Professor Maciej Luniak rightly points out that the function of city parks has changed since the time we were turned on by a viewing axis. In the nineteenth century the inhabitants of Warsaw didn't go to the Łazienki Gardens to take a break from the city's noise. They strolled the park to point up their social status, exchange polite bows, at most to engage in refined conversation. Admission was refused to the poor and the wrongly dressed – in a word, those who would have spoiled the idyll of the elite. Twenty-first century customs, though, are rather more democratic, and users of green spaces are above all seeking tranquillity. People today are said to want contact with nature. Why don't they notice it and fight for it in the city?

Why is the design of green space governed by 'nice' in its most primitive meaning? The layered structure of vegetation specific to our climate is reduced to its topmost and bottommost strata. Bushes are mercilessly uprooted because they're a burden to look after and they're associated with neglect. 'Brush', the proponents of 'nice' say in disgust. But nature fights back and, every spring, frail stalks push up through the unevenly laid concrete paving blocks. Moss grows green by the drainage grates, while blue chicory flourishes along the bike paths. A tiny aspen, missed by the mowers, glitters in the sun.

5 February

Urban birds are much less shy than their wild cousins. Species living in parks have what is known as a reduced flight zone. A woodland blackbird will start up noisily and flee at the very sight of a human. The same is true of mallards, which in parks are known for their begging. Any birder will tell you that in the wild they're only ever seen flying away, driven off by the presence of people. The more relaxed character of urban birds enables us to observe their unusual behaviours. The most fun is surely provided by the corvids, with their wise-guy leer, their calculated brazenness and their skill in disembowelling plastic rubbish sacks. Today in the Pole Mokotowskie Park, I saw a crow holding some white object in its bill. At first I thought it was a pigeon egg, but the crow alighted on the asphalt and let go of its treasure. It turned out to be a golf ball. The creature watched closely as the strange egg rolled slowly across the path. Its peculiar movement evidently intrigued the bird. The ball now speeded up, now slowed down as it encountered unseen dips and bumps or dropped into shallow ruts formed by the folds in the asphalt. In the end it came to a stop. The bird waited a moment then began the game all over again.

23 March

The famous pair of peregrine falcons in the Bielany neighbourhood of Warsaw – Franek and Leśna – have laid their first egg. Their nest is an unusual one; it's on a balcony on the fourteenth floor of a high-rise apartment building. I like the Bielany falcons because they don't look down on the ant-like humans from 120 metres up, like the conceited pair from the Palace of Culture. The Bielany couple lead the life of ordinary Varsovians – they live in a tower block. An internet camera has been set up next to their nest and it can be watched around the clock. Birdwatching in front of the computer is an excellent exercise in relaxation – either one of the falcons is there or it isn't. It sits, or it busies itself with something. Sometimes there's fog and nothing can be seen. The pair are fascinating. The male is ringed, which means he's from the reintroduction programme; the female has nothing on her leg, showing that she's from the wild. Love is clearly blind, even when it comes to falcons. The two birds have a large following. People send one another screenshots: Leśna with a bat she's caught; Franek scratching his ear; Franek after it's been raining (he looks like a drenched chicken). But the fixed camera doesn't show us what we most admire them for: their hunting.

It was by that apartment block in Bielany that I observed my only falcon hunt in Warsaw. The bird soared up, intent on some point invisible to me; with a few strong wing-beats it rose to the necessary height, then dropped like a stone at extraordinary speed behind some trees. I didn't witness the moment when it dug its talons into its victim, then snatched it up as it fell to the ground. I saw only the beginning of the operation and its grand finale. A few minutes later the falcon reappeared, gripping a blackbird. It perched on the edge of the roof of its building and in the rays of the setting sun began plucking the dead bird's feathers. It looked as if it was marking the end of the show by showering us with confetti.

In the mid-nineteenth century Władysław Taczanowski, the father of Polish ornithology, also observed falcons in Warsaw. He wrote for instance of a female:

…who in autumn regularly comes to the city and spends entire days on the cornices of the Church of the Holy Cross and the Carmelite Church on Krakowskie Przedmieście. Paying no attention to the commotion and clamour of the city, or the constant presence of passers-by, she perches there tranquil as can be, dozing, then she preens, being at the greatest ease in this place which is safe for her. Generally around ten o'clock in the morning she fetches herself a pigeon, which she plucks with all the calm in the world, then tears apart amid a gathering audience of city dwellers eager for entertainment. Boys sometimes throw pebbles at her; they shout, clap their hands, and try various means of scaring her off; the bird pays no attention and continues what she is doing.

30 March
Franek and Leśna now have four eggs.

21 April
The brazen squirrels climb up the tourists' trouser legs. There's Tosia the tame deer. Peacocks' cries echo all the way across the park, and they puff themselves up to have their photo taken in front of the Palace on the Water. Apparently a fox ate one of those narcissists and as a punishment was evicted with its entire family. I believe in the fact that it was an eviction. I always look for tawny owls. They're sometimes to be found on the tree with the broken crown, or by the Orangery. This spring four downy chicks were reared, and now they sit meekly high on the branch of a spruce tree. It's hard to see them from the ground; it took me ten or fifteen minutes of shifting my position and peering through my binoculars before I found them.

At the foot of the tree are pellets – undigested parts of eaten animals. They have the disagreeable shape of cylindrical dumplings. I took one home and let it sit in warm water. What I had taken to be mouse or vole fur turned out to be a condensed mass of feathers, and tiny bones eaten away by stomach acids – a source of calcium for the owls. If they fed exclusively on meat, their skeleton would be soft and misshapen. What had the owls consumed? A small leg with a claw looked like that of a robin, which I've seen close up, but it could have been some other small species. In recent years in the Łazienki Gardens a large number of bushes have been cleared; long-time visitors say there are far fewer birds. Where snowberries, yews or euonymus remain, robins can be heard chirping in the evening.

6 May

A few days ago three of Franek and Leśna's eggs hatched. It seems that nothing will come of the fourth egg.

8 May

The Bird Patrol is a group of volunteers who, under the leadership of Renata Markowska, fight for urban birds' right to exist. Today for the first time this spring we took action in the case of the heating duct work being carried out in the Praga neighbourhood. Openings in the flat roofs have been grated over, and the swifts were unable to gain access to their nests from last year. Their habitat is legally protected (the Protection of Nature Act and the Ordinance of the Ministry for the Environment of 6 October, 2014), and the building management does not have official permission to destroy it. But managers routinely ignore the law; in addition, the fines are risible. Residents rarely protest, and usually in vain. Naturalists often look away, for the struggle is an onerous and thankless one and, after all, the city birds are in no danger of extinction. The entire breeding season for Renata means endless trips from one end of the city to the other. All day long. Four months of frayed nerves, of wrangling in government offices and arguments with managements.

We tip our heads back. The swifts with their black crescent-shaped wings cut through the air with a piercing whistle. Cries from hundreds of throats rise in the quiet evening sky. It will be the loveliest sound of the city summer. The rushing squadrons will vie with one another, as in Giacomo Balla's painting *Swifts: Paths of Movement + Dynamic Sequences*. The dark curve of a shape repeated over and over in an easy line, as in a blurred photograph. The trajectory of one is superimposed on the flight paths of other birds. Dynamism, abruptness, and at the same time fluidity of movement. The Polish title of the painting is *The Flight of the Swallow*, but swifts, though similar, are not related to swallows. While we were walking around the outside of the building, the heating workers slashed the tyres of my bicycle.

May 11

I take a look outside a small apartment block in the Ochota neighbourhood where J. and M. live. The heating work has been done on a third of the building already, and there are sparrows everywhere. Four nests behind the gutter, one beneath a windowsill, two behind another gutter. I go up to the foreman and, striving to adopt an official tone, I say: 'Good morning. There are sparrows' nests on the building, the work has to be stopped.' The guy looks at me good-naturedly and says: 'I know, I know, we're not doing anything right now, and the ornithologist will be here this afternoon.' I don't believe him. A polite man called Mr Przemek, one of the workers, speaks up, saying he made a note of the phone number. The ornithologist is called Mariusz. 'What's his last name?' I ask, because maybe I know him. 'Mariusz Ornithologist,' Mr Przemek smiles. I call, and it really is an ornithologist. He's aware of the situation already, but he'll come by anyway, take a look and make an assessment. I decide to take a photo of the van belonging to this unusual building company that cares about sparrows. I get out my camera, and here some guy comes running. His neck's stuck out, his arms are held stiffly alongside his body.

'What's this, eh? What do you need pictures for, eh? That's

my van, I don't want any pictures taken, eh? Eh?'

'I wanted to give you some publicity, sir, to tell people you're not walling up the sparrows.'

'Eh? Eh?' He blinks distractedly. 'Oh, all right. I thought it was because we parked on the grass, but we're allowed to, the grass belongs to the housing cooperative, eh?'

16 May

Today work on a heating system upgrade is being done in the Wola neighbourhood. Two other volunteers and I help Dorota the ornithologist check the building. Within a couple of minutes we see house sparrows and tree sparrows flying into the vents. On another wall, at the place where the air conditioning cables enter the building, a blue tit has built a nest. Any ornithologist preparing an assessment of the modernisation of an apartment building's heating system ought to conduct the inspection during the breeding season (unfortunately, not all of them can be bothered). If the birds turn out to have laid eggs, the work has to be halted. After a few minutes two guys walk up to us assertively. Self-important types from the housing cooperative.

'Ms Dorota, we're starting to get tired of this!' the younger one exclaims. They paid for an ornithological assessment, not an inspection once the work is under way. The older one complains in a Warsaw drawl: 'Hooow much do you want? It's briiibery! Hooow much more are you gonna take us for?' He's unable to comprehend that people can work on the protection of nature voluntarily, in their free time. Dorota won't let the matter go till the sparrows are able to raise their young in peace. It's also necessary to ensure that nesting boxes are put up here after the season as part of the so-called compensation (though the word 'recompense' would seem more appropriate).

25 May

Sometimes I wonder what Warsaw looks like through the eyes of a bird. Perhaps for them the city is a part of the natural landscape? Mountain chains of estates, windswept crags of tower blocks, and the gentle hills of older apartment complexes. Wild, moss-covered cliffs of unoccupied buildings. Deep canyons of streets. Cliff ledges of balconies and windowsills. Overgrown steppes of empty lots. Rock-strewn building sites. Prairies of railroad sidings. Jungle along the river. Lianas of streetcar cables. Oases of squares, wadis of drainage ditches. Little pools in the cracked asphalt. Waterfalls from fountains. Ponds, clay pits, lakes. The last major wild river in Europe.

Life in the city requires flexibility. You have to get used to constant changes in the lie of the land. To the perpetual presence of humans. To street lamps and twenty-four-hour traffic. But then there are conveniences to be grateful for. There aren't many predators, and the food supply is plentiful (especially for those that avail themselves of trash). Many species moved into the city only very recently. Blackbirds, for example, didn't appear in Warsaw city centre till the 1960s. Magpies moved in not much earlier. The process of adapting to the city environment is called synurbisation.

1 June

Dziki Zakątek ('Wild Corner') in the Pole Mokotowskie Park. The city is planning to create a dog run here, with obstacles, tunnels and a pond. Officially it's said that twenty-six trees are to be felled, but in reality it could be as many as four times that number. Many plum trees and apple trees grow here that were in the former allotment gardens. Unfortunately, by law fruit trees can be cut down with impunity. No one consulted the local residents about these plans. No one assessed the natural value of the place, and I'd lay down good money that no official ever bothered to actually visit. The Office of Environmental Protection, which has approved the project, says in addition that the trees in the dog run will be disinfected. The officials are afraid of dog pee. Wildlife has no right to survive here.

In the opinion of one biologist involved in the case, in terms of nature Dziki Zakątek is one of the most valuable places in the park. Paweł and I have come to count and map the nests of birds. My companion, a professional ornithologist, has led workshops for children here, and he already knows the place well. Although the season is unfavourable (leaves already conceal the tops of the trees), in the space of half an hour we find as many as seventeen nests from the previous year. It's an impressive figure for such a small area; it's hard to know how many we've missed. There are nests of fieldfare (eight), great tit (two), blue tit (two), starling (two), hooded crow (two) and one unidentified one. Since hawfinches have been around all spring, their nests must be here as well, hidden behind the curtain of foliage.

Most urban birds build their nests in the fruit trees and ashleaf maples that the officials scorn above all else. The latter are particularly unloved. 'Invasive species,' they mutter at City Hall, as if they were speaking of some shameful disease. Maybe for dendrologists they're less precious trees, but they withstand drought, as well as the wintertime salting of the pavements. And they grow everywhere. The birds don't complain either – ashleaf maples and fruit trees have many natural hollows. The most interesting nest is one belonging to a fieldfare. It's less than a metre from the ground, built on a metal post that has grown into the tree. In the city birds will make use of any suitable spot. They lay their eggs on picket fences, in the locks of gates, on street lamps. They're not fussy.

9 June

A concrete retention pond in Pole Mokotowskie Park. A dog, let's call it Fifi, for the past quarter of an hour has been swimming after a duck with three ducklings. The bird doesn't rise into the air but stays ushering its offspring along. The owner calls half-heartedly from the bank: 'Fifi, Fifi!' Fifi, intent on the duck, is on her eighth circuit of the pond. Two sporty-looking young guys are looking on. One of them finally loses patience. 'For f—k's sake, man, take your trousers off and get in the water!' He can't bear to see the poor duck suffering like that, he explains to his pal and me. The owner of the dog flinches, but a moment later he brings out the big guns: 'You can't talk to someone like that, I'll call the police!' As if on command, two officers appear from behind a tree. 'We got a report that you're setting your dog on ducks. Get in the water, sir.' The young guys are triumphant, the bristling owner makes a performance of taking off one grey sock at a time. He rolls up his trouser-legs and wades into the pond. Fifi comes to her senses. The two of them clamber out of the water. On the bank, the fine is being written up.

A female mallard duck with her ducklings

30 June

Zbyszek runs an infirmary for animals in his one-room apartment. Hedgehogs hit by cars, wounded birds, chicks thrown out of their nest – they all end up here. At first I'm given the tasks of a beginning volunteer. I have to clean the cages, wash away the droppings, feathers and leftover food. Turn over the towels used as lining. Smelliest of all are the cages with two long-eared owls. The older one is fierce; it puffs itself up and rocks from side to side. It snaps its beak and lashes out at me with its talons whenever I put my hand in the cage. The other owl is quieter. I take it out of its cage like a chicken and place it on the carpet. It stands there patiently and watches what I'm doing, with its big yellow eyes. It has a wound on its wing which has gone bad; now the festering tissue needs to be disinfected. Also, something is wrong with one of its eyes. I give each owl a chicken heart and a mouse embryo.

'Even as a child I brought home rooks and jackdaws that I'd found,' Zbyszek tells me. 'They mostly died, because I didn't know how to take care of them. I learned from my own mistakes. In Poland there's no professional literature explaining how to look after a bird. When someone finds one and decides to rescue it, they ought to be aware that there's an institution they can turn to for help. I never say no to anyone, but some folks drive me nuts. My phone number is widely available, and people think I'm some kind of telephone information service or that I have sixty people working for me, with branches all over the country. They don't understand that I can't come to where they are, because I myself have to feed fifty birds.

'Some of them get upset when I'm not charming and

engaging, and I don't jump in my helicopter at the drop of a hat to remove a jackdaw nest from their chimney in central Poland. Yet there are others who are grateful for information on where birds can be taken, or what to feed them. They listen, take notes, learn. Though there are always strange stories. This season's winner was someone who found a young rook and fed it strawberries – yes, rooks are omnivores, but within reason. I once got some blue tit chicks that some lady had given milk for kittens. I guess she was thinking of the sweet that's called *ptasie mleczko* or bird's milk.'

1 July

A thrush that some people had decided to save on their own has found its way to Zbyszek's. The bird had a broken wing, and its finders did not give it a splint. They thought it would heal by itself. The thrush will never fly again; it'll end up at a special centre in Mikołów where it will spend the rest of its life. Zbyszek doesn't like feeding it, because it's always a mad struggle. The thrush 'is demanding its right to death by starvation'. Yesterday there were also problems with a blind starling chick. Its intestines were blocked. The emergency lasted till four in the morning. After consulting with a vet, Zbyszek bought paraffin at an all-night pharmacy. He wasn't feeding the chick, only giving it liquids. In the morning it shat out a knot of tapeworms. Now it demands food constantly. A tiny little starling like that is a bottomless sack. When it grows up, it too will be sent to Mikołów. There, in the company of other starlings, it will learn how to be a starling.

'I wouldn't want people to get the impression that I lead some kind of magical life among the birds,' Zbyszek says. 'All this is not normal. From May to August I'm completely isolated here. I go to sleep at four or five in the morning, I get up before nine. I feed the birds. I spend my whole day immersed in droppings, insects, meat. I have to disinfect myself all the time. I'm forever cleaning up and fighting to reduce the stench. I eat breakfast at two in the afternoon. That's also when I can answer my e-mails – which mostly involves giving the addresses of places that take in animals. I feed the birds again. Chicks are supposed to eat every hour, I'm perpetually behind. I turn over the towels that line the cages. I buy frozen food. I eat dinner-cum-supper at ten in the evening.

'A few years down the line I'll find out about work-related illnesses. I don't think I have any parasites. In August my back aches because I have dozens of swifts to feed. I spend hours sitting down and leaning forward. Though at least at those times I can look at my laptop. During the breeding season I sleep four hours a night, so in the winter I catch up on my sleep with a clear conscience. Last year I went to bed in mid-October and got up two weeks later. I'd wake every twelve hours or so, eat something, and go back to sleep. I'd sleep as much as twenty hours a day. At the beginning of November I felt like I'd caught up and I could go back to work.'

13 July

Warsaw is of course a metropolis on a national scale, but think of true urban giants. New York for instance. A megalopolis of concrete, glass, and steel. You'd think that being a naturalist in a place like that was the most frustrating thing in the world.

Manhattan's Appalachia of skyscrapers and the canyons of streets all at right angles. Who'd have thought that in the land of Woody Allen and Lou Reed there existed life other than the social kind? And yet: during bird migrations New York is a mecca for urban ornithologists. The city lies between two major rivers, at the edge of the ocean. Millions of birds have been flying that way for thousands of years, and their path didn't change just because of the sudden appearance of skyscrapers. Many birds don't only fly over New York, but also pause there to regain their strength. Why? Because of the huge green island in the middle of the city.

Central Park came into being in the nineteenth century. It occupies over 800 acres. Even though it's surrounded by a monster of a city, in certain places it's retained a surprisingly wild character. Peering upwards on a regular basis in Manhattan can allow you to see as many as 200 bird species. Over the course of several decades, Starr Saphir spotted 259 species in Central Park alone. She was the guru of many generations of New York birders. She died in 2013 of a cancer that she'd been battling for eleven years. Even during her chemotherapy, two or three times a week she'd lead birding tours through the park. If there were a lot of birds, the tours could last up to six hours. Bent over, walking with evident difficulty, during that time Saphir would take only two short breaks. The fee was eight dollars, and the walks continued almost until the day she died.

14 August

A red sun climbs slowly from behind the woods across the river. Today it slept near Józefów. A misty cloud drifts over the surface of the water; shapes slowly emerge from the damp haze. A grim heron like a grey knight in a drab cloak stands motionless on a sandbank. Through my binoculars I watch ruff wading in the pools of the disappearing river. Their unremarkable brown plumage looks nothing like the extravagant puffed-up collars they had in May, from which they take their English name. It's as if you were dealing with an entirely different species. At their feet a squat little common sandpiper wanders about, flicking its tail incessantly. It's like a little pudgy child. Far away on a spit of sand, five turnstones are sounding the mud – they've made a short stopover on the way to their wintering grounds. In the meantime M. lies down on the icy sand and conceals himself with a tarpaulin. He'll lie there with his camera trained on the shallows near the water's edge, while I walk on so as not to scare his birds away.

10 September

The freeway through Warsaw's Wola district is lined with soundproofing screens. At the foot of one green barrier the body of a young cuckoo is lying on its belly. I take a stick to turn over its rigid form. I hold my breath, expecting the stink of decaying flesh and a writhing mass of larvae at work on the flesh, but the cuckoo is only an emptied-out shell – it weighs no more than the feathers covering it and the hollow bones. The rest has been completely eaten away. Researchers estimate that every year in America between 300,000 and a billion birds die from flying into the windows and walls of buildings. In Poland research of that kind has not been carried out on a large scale. The outlines of falcons and ravens stuck on the screens fail to scare off passing birds. Apparently what works are grilles embedded in the plexiglass that reflect UV rays, which are visible to birds. They're slowly starting to appear in Poland.

8 October

David Lindo is a well-known British city birdwatcher. In his inspiring book *The Urban Birder* he sets out his birdwatching philosophy: 'Simply look up.' *The Urban Birder* is not only the author's birding credo, but also the fascinating story of a passion. Lindo had been interested in birds since his earliest childhood, which he spent in the north-eastern suburbs of London. He describes endearingly his first sightings, including the typical mistakes and dilemmas of the beginning ornithologist. The thorough exploration of the neighbourhood, walking about with his eyes permanently raised, hours spent poring over his bird book. And the conviction that the most interesting places are not neatly trimmed lawns and immaculate flowerbeds but brush, and everything that brings a grimace to the face of town-dwelling pedants.

Lindo decided that birdwatching in cities needed to be given its due. For many of us, tower blocks and city streets are gradually becoming a natural environment. It's generally accepted that by 2050 almost three quarters of the earth's population will be living in cities. Meanwhile, even the commonest urban bird species – when they're shown to those who have no idea they're there – are a source of genuine delight. People should be taught that nature is everywhere and that it needs our help. It's best to begin with small things: raising awareness of the vital role played by lawns covered in springtime dandelions, by tangled scrub in parks, or by fruit trees that have reverted to the wild state. If it can be explained why Dziki Zakątek in the Pole Mokotowskie Park should be preserved, then the necessity of protecting priceless thousand-year-old ecosystems will be obvious, right?

5 November

Staszek sent me a film of a woodcock walking about in his apartment. It looks exactly like a kiwi: a small, stubby creature with short legs and a long bill. Staszek found it near Unii Lubelskiej Square; he kept it overnight then turned it in to the Bird Sanctuary at Warsaw Zoo. The bird had been on its way to its wintering grounds when it crashed into the window of some building. In the film it doesn't look badly injured. Maybe in a few days it'll get its strength back and continue on its flight? The woodcock is a curious bird. Its beak is a sensitive probe used for finding invertebrates in the earth. It's surprisingly soft to the touch. The woodcock has trouble seeing what's in front of it – its big convex eyes are placed on either side of its head. This arrangement has its advantages: it produces a wide field of vision which makes it hard for predators to sneak up. It evidently did not see the window panes that were straight ahead. We usually see woodcock in the spring during their 'roding' or courtship flights. At such times the males fly very slowly just above the crowns of the trees, emitting the strangest snorting and clicking sounds.

9 November

I visit the tawny owls in Mokotów Park. Whenever I look up in search of the familiar puffy forms, someone notices and strikes up a conversation. 'They're not there, I already looked. First thing I do when I'm in the park, I check if the owls are there,' says a drunk walking his dog, with a beaming smile. A spry elderly lady offers advice: 'I had a spare moment so I've come to see whether they're up there. If the grey one isn't by the broken branch, it'll be in the big lime tree by the palace.' Indeed, there it is. If it hadn't been for the tip I'd probably have missed it. I stand at the foot of the tree, and for a moment the owl opens its eyes. It peers grudgingly down from above. I don't look like anything of interest. After a short while it goes back to its interrupted nap.

3 December

By the garages on Sanocka Street I see the flash of a ruddy tail. The black redstart likes building sites, rubble, the treeless centres of towns – in a word, places that resemble the tumble of rocks at the foot of cliffs in the high mountains. That used to be its home, from which it set out to conquer the lowlands. A few years ago, on Zawrat in the Tatra Mountains, I heard its rattling song. It was the only bird to be heard in a labyrinth of granite blocks two kilometres above the level of the Baltic. Several hundred metres below, the Valley of the Five Lakes had been alive with the song of water pipits and dunnocks, and in the dwarf mountain pines common redpolls were hopping about. In the silence of the rocky wilderness the black redstart was alone. Only once the piercing whistle of a marmot, the mountain squirrel, sounded.

Most black redstarts fly south in the autumn, but each year there are individuals who attempt to winter in the city.

The one on Sanocka Street will be looking for invertebrates on the warmed walls of buildings and by ventilation ducts. But when the frosts come it'll have a really hard time of it. Who knows, maybe it'll head south after all? Last year, a coal-black individual wintered by the National Library. Two weeks of freezing temperatures towards the end of January were tough for it, so I fed it a bit with insects I bought at the fishing store. It survived.

A STORK CALLED STONELIS

It's only 10 a.m., but the car is already an oven. The imitation leather steering wheel first burns, then sticks to the hands. The hot air slowly escapes through the half-opened windows. In the morning new bodies are always to be found on the road; today, by the roadside there's a red fox that's been hit by some vehicle. The creature is lifeless – it's the wind that is moving its bushy tail. A friend of mine collects such roadkill, lays it out in front of his hide and waits for predators with his camera. But even if I wanted to pick the fox up for him, first, the seats of my car are strewn with maps, tables and directions; second, the police could arrest me for poaching; and, third, I'm facing a whole day of driving in the heat. Besides, I used up a lot of early morning energy on making myself look respectable. I don't want to get covered in blood now. I'm going to be counting storks' nests in Grabów District on the Pilica River.

Graduate in German, nature activist, lover of the Tatra Mountains. The first person to reach the summit of Świnica. A Catholic priest who later abandoned the cassock, started a family and became a Protestant pastor. Eugeniusz Janota, man of many abilities, towards the end of his life in 1876 decided to count the number of storks in the Austrian partition zone. To this end, by way of the educational journals *Szkoła* and *Gazeta Szkolna* he asked country teachers for information about birds nesting in their area. As he had carefully calculated, his appeal was able to reach 3,000 readers. Only 176 replied, including, as he himself emphasised, thirty-five Ruthenians. 'The reports sent in by these teachers were in the great majority of cases submitted eagerly and accurately, for which I hereby express my gratitude.'

Poland joined the international stork census in 1934. Since that time birds and nests have been counted more or less every decade. More or less, because during the war no one had much enthusiasm for the task. Documenting birds by the so-called 'partisan method' could take an unexpected turn. With notebook and binoculars in hand, the counter would no doubt have been mistaken for a spy or saboteur. In the stormy post-war years too there were more pressing things to do than go looking for storks. In the sixties also, for reasons unknown to me, no count took place.

Grabów District begins on the other side of the bridge in Warka. The landscape is entirely different from that on this side of the Pilica, with its high banks. The country is flat, agricultural, poor. There are no fruit trees or paved courtyards such as are found among the apple barons of Grójec District. Late July is the last moment for the count, as the birds could already have left the nest. On the way I see stork parents walking with their young in the meadows. Best of all is to begin by asking the owner of the house where the nest is: how many chicks were there? Did they all survive? Are there other storks in the neighbourhood? In the village of Kępa Niemojewska everyone says there's one nest with three young.

From previous counts I know that the nest has existed here for at least twenty years. The stork youngsters are eating something the adult bird has brought them, but a moment later they all fly off in different directions. Following instructions, I write down in the table: TPCC (telegraph pole, concrete, circular), MP (metal platform), HPY3 (three young); state of nest: poor (and in the comments section: nest too big). For at least twenty years the birds have been adding new twigs to the pile, so little wonder the construction is so huge. It's happened that nests like this, compacted and cemented with mud, weighing several hundred kilograms, have come crashing down through roofs.

Throughout the Slavic lands a stork's nest was always a good omen. It was said to protect the occupants of the house from lightning and fire. The bird itself, of course, is a symbol of fertility. After all, it appears when the deadness of winter is retreating, and the earth is ready to yield up its fruits once again. The stork's wings are 'spring's first flag', writes Adam Mickiewicz. And of course the stork brings children. Usually it drops them down the chimney (with the playful connotation of a dark opening and a red phallic bill). Storks have lived alongside people for centuries, so it's hardly surprising they've been given human traits. In ancient Greece, then later in Rome, it was believed that they look after their old infirm progenitors. That's why the obligation to care for one's parents is called the *lex ciconaria*, or stork's law.

This is the last remaining nest in Kępa Niemojewska, while twenty years ago there were three. A hundred years ago there were probably over a dozen, maybe even several times that many. I think the whole area must have looked a little like a Chełmoński painting. In the spring the Pilica used to flood extensively, and herds of patient cows used to graze in the meadows. Storks like their meadows trimmed short; in high grass it's hard for them to see their prey – small mammals, reptiles, amphibians, young birds. But cows are hard to come by these days; only a few people keep them, out of habit. And mowing meadows isn't really worth the effort. Pastureland becomes overgrown. Land that used to be marshy has been drained, sown and probably given up on long ago. Also, the river hardly floods any more.

The ancient legend went more or less as follows: when the Lord God created the world – all the thistles, the ticks and the people – and on the seventh day he was resting, he noticed that in his perfect garden a mass of revolting things were proliferating: slimy amphibians, reptiles, bugs. Everything that crawls, rubbing its belly against the earth, is close to the darkness and the Devil. Humans also do not rise from the ground, and for that reason must fight for their own salvation. So God rolled up his sleeves one more time, went down to earth and gathered all the disgusting creatures in a sack. (Here we must ask: how can we fail to believe we were made in his image? We too like to put things in our own kind of order. We use Roundup to kill off the cornflowers, tansy and especially those pesky dandelions.)

But coming back to God: He handed the vermin in the sack to a man he trusted and told him to throw it in the water. Drown everything. Like puppies that multiply so wantonly in the country. Yet God was evidently mistaken about the man he had created, for the latter had no intention of disposing of the sack so quickly. The Lord God's rubbish might be some pretty good stuff! he thought, and slapped his thigh in delight because he smelled profit. He opened up the sack; but before he could even stick his head inside, all the toads, newts and snakes came crawling out.

They scattered in the grass, and the man stood watching with his mouth stupidly agape. God was angered. 'From now on till the end of the world you'll be gathering up what you let out, you fool,' he said; he waved his hand, and the man turned into a stork. Or rather, into a stork prototype that still had a human voice, and so he began to protest. He complained, appealed to non-existent laws and conventions, but the Lord God had lost patience with him. Another moment and there'd have been no more bird. Yet God thought: There's no point in destroying something that's just been created. So he decided instead to take the stork's tongue away. Since that time, the creature has only been able to clatter its bill. It's a sad story, because it traces the stork back to some shady wise-guy. Apparently, according to Ludwik Adam Jucewicz, a scholar of Lithuanian folklore, the man's name was Stonelis.

A crew is plastering a house in apricot and, though I'm a little afraid of being made fun of, I ask if they know anything about storks in the area. Indeed they do; with a friendly smile they tell me that in a nest in Łękawica village two birds have survived and are sitting on the dead body of their brother. Most of the workmen are not from around here, so they don't know any more. Only one of them is from the village, but he snorts angrily. 'Storks! Like I care!' He's the touchy type. In the meantime it's cooling off and grey clouds are covering the sky.

In Zakrzew things have got worse too. In 1994 there were two nests here, now there's only one. Two young birds have been reared, but one egg and one grown chick were thrown out by the parents. People can't understand this or forgive it. Yet a sick, verminous chick is a danger to its siblings. One that's crippled or undersized is another hungry mouth to feed, and sooner or later it will die anyway. Instinct tells the parents that in nature there's no place for the sick or the infirm. 'Perhaps among these birds the principles of the Spartans of old hold sway, for it is above all the sickly young that encounter this sorry fate,' Janota speculates.

And the egg that was tossed out? Perhaps it was unincubated or had been cracked in the course of some scuffle. Storks often fight over nests in good spots. Here the location is proven; it might not be able to support two nests, but one for sure. There's a river close by, and fields containing rodents just across the fence. In the season, an adult stork moves heaven and earth to feed its young. Every day it spends over ten hours chasing around after the spillings of the sack. For four young, the adult couple can bring up to three kilograms of food daily. In the first days of life their offspring is fed with worms. Along with earth from the worms' digestive tracts, the chicks ingest heavy metals (analysis of young birds reveals much about pollution levels in a given area). Later, incidentally, they assimilate them from the bodies of rodents, reptiles, amphibians and insects. Storks do not debone their victims but rather swallow them whole, for without the calcium from their bones and feathers the storks' skeletons would be weak and brittle. Like owls, in their stomach they form cylindrical pellets from the undigested leftovers. The pellets contain what's left of the creatures they've eaten – the exoskeletons of insects and the bones of vertebrates.

A farmer's wife in Grabów Zaleśny has taken in a chick thrown out of the nest and fed it live fish, as recommended. Her grandson catches them in some pond, and the stork fishes them out of a bucket. It's just eaten; it looks at us, tips its head sideways, raises its wings and hisses. 'That shows it's pleased,' says the grandson, who looks like a little Linnaeus. The adult couple are still raising three young, so they have their red hands full; the fourth one was probably the weakest.

The bird walks around the farmyard all day long; it flies up a little, and it chases the cat, which keeps getting in its way. It looks good and healthy – in other words, it's made up for its shortcomings. But the stork family, whose nest is fifteen metres away, pay no attention to it. The farmer's wife worries about what will happen in the winter. She can't bring it into the house; besides, the stork has a huge appetite, and feeding it is expensive. I suggest that she put the bird in a cardboard box and take it to the Warsaw Zoo. In the autumn, though, I learn that at the last minute the young stork re-joined its kin and flew off in an unknown direction. The wooden pole (WP) on

A pair of nesting storks

which the nest rests is crooked and rotten; it urgently needs to be replaced, before it collapses onto a newly constructed fence.

I don't understand why, among Chełmoński's many splendid paintings, *Storks* is the most popular of all. It's probably because of the subject matter – after all, the stork is our unofficial national emblem. But when I look at that mawkish, folksy landscape, I see only the artificiality of the scene it depicts. Why is the old ploughman digging into his lunch with his legs straight out? It's hard to imagine a less comfortable position to eat in, especially because his back must ache from the ploughing. And why are they eating in full sunlight? I can't believe there's no pear tree growing somewhere on a field boundary. And the storks crossing the sky aren't particularly well executed either.

Ten years ago in Wyborów there was an old nest that had been abandoned by three young. Some storks appeared here this spring too, but the neighbours drove them away. 'They said they'd shoot them because the storks were frightening away their pigeons,' one local lady says in a whisper, tapping her forehead to indicate the people are mad. 'Someone ought to call the police. You're not allowed to scare birds away from their own nest,' she declares, but then smiles as if she were talking to a pre-schooler. 'Oh no, I'd never hear the end of it.'

Harassing storks, destroying their nest, and especially

killing them, was in many cultures regarded as a mortal sin. In the Mazowsze region the culprit could expect to lose his son. There was also a popular superstition claiming that storks took revenge by setting light to a thatched roof (they could spark fire with their bills) They were apparently also able to bring about an uninterrupted deluge that made the hay rot, or a lengthy drought that would leave the earth a cracked crust. Or a one-off mighty hailstorm that flattened entire fields of grain.

The guys at the roadside chapel are well informed too. They know of nests in Broncin and Łękawica. I rarely have that reassuring feeling that people are good after all. The men are glad there are still storks living in the area, and worried that their numbers are decreasing. But I don't think that for that reason they'd be willing to spread fewer chemicals on their fields and go back to the laborious old methods of farming. After half an hour of traipsing here and there along dirt tracks, hearing the chassis clattering, I reach Broncin. Two young on an isolated concrete pole. On a barn roof there's a platform prepared for another nest, as thought up by the farmer. 'My husband's full of ideas,' a lady in a flower-patterned headscarf says proudly.

The sun comes out, it gets hot again, and the roadside crickets spring to life. A Montagu's harrier passes low over the grass; higher up, a hobby with its curved wings is catching insects. In Łękawica, the promised nest is next to the presbytery. One young bird is standing in it; the other is probably out in the fields with its parents. The one I'm watching is probably the weaker one, since the adults keep bringing it food. In the nest I can see the black wing of a dead chick flicking with every gust of wind. It's odd that the parents didn't throw out the corpse – a decaying body is very dangerous. Maybe the bird got tangled in some string brought to the nest? That's often the cause of death or injury in young storks.

In Łękawica there's also a nest by the fish ponds, and in it there are three young birds. The village isn't even mentioned in the counts of 1994 and 2004. So it's not entirely true that the storks of Grabów District have no hope. The nest by the ponds is also home to at least one pair of tree sparrows, those country cousins of the house sparrow. Squatters are no rarity – such massive constructions have all kinds of nooks and crannies. As many as fourteen different species have been recorded as making use of storks' nests, from sparrows and wagtails, through blackbirds, to individual cases of a nesting mallard and even a kestrel. The tree sparrows of Łękawica know what they're about, for a few dozen metres away are some stables offering a rich source of oats and of flies.

In 1899, just before *Storks*, Chełmoński painted *Haystack in the Pińsk Region*, a picture of elegant simplicity. It's noteworthy for its nostalgic mood and the warm colours of a clear summer evening. A quietly flowing river, a haystack partly underwater, and on it a stork which, turning away from the viewer, is preening. Pink evening cumulus clouds are reflected in the current. Chełmoński placed the horizon low, so the calming sky dominates. There's so much air in the painting that you can almost smell the river and the adjoining meadows. I'd be glad to have an eastern stork like that on my wall – intimate, immersed in the landscape, alone.

Utniki is situated on a truly ugly, monotonous flatland. Once again, three young storks are in the nest, which has been there for at least twenty years. The gate is open, the dog looks at me unamicably, but it doesn't bark. I walk into the farmyard and call self-consciously: 'Hello? Hello?' No one responds. The house door is invitingly ajar so I step inside, and there an elderly man on a couch eyes me abstractedly. Next to him, a glass of cold tea in a metal holder rests on an oilcloth covering the table. I ask falteringly about storks, but he speaks indistinctly, staring at the walls with a glassy look. I retreat and leave in hopes that I won't encounter some suspicious daughter or aggressive son-in-law.

Utniki turns imperceptibly into Grabina; the change of locality is marked only by a road sign. Here the district record is set: four young. The farmer's a little disgruntled because in the spring the storks were on the point of being disloyal to him; they started to build a nest two telegraph poles down, at his neighbours'. But for some reason it didn't work out, and they came back. 'What was wrong with our place?' he asks indignantly in the direction of the pole.

'But they did come back, they're here now, right?' I feel strangely like the storks' advocate. People give them names, get attached to them, are upset at them, forgive them, get sentimental about them. In Karwik in the Masurian Lakes there was a stork named Kuba, who lived at a campground. Every year when we went there we'd see him strolling decorously across the field behind the house. Alas, one spring Kuba met his end. The poor thing got his feet caught in a medium-tension wire and caused a short circuit. Apparently everyone was devastated – the holidaymakers, the locals, even the guys that work the lock on the Jegliński Canal.

Janota wrote extensively about marital infidelity among storks. About jealousy, family quarrels, but also about attachment. He recounted the following story, for instance:

In 1847 in Prokocim a storm blew down part of the nest of a pair of storks that had been known there for many years. Two incubated eggs were broken, and two chicks killed. In spring 1848 the same pair returned, but the birds were despondent; they spent day and night standing or sitting by one another, and did so with such loving caresses and such affectionate embraces! They would always go to seek food together, always fly back together; they were always sad and silent, never clattering their bills … In that year of mourning they had no offspring. It was only in 1849 that, with a loud clatter, the stork announced to those listening that he had become a father.

Fortunately, stork meat is not very good. In his sixteenth-century *Hunting with Birds* Mateusz Cygański, the great-grandfather of Polish ornithology, described this fact in verse:

> It is a household bird: the stork performs
> The task of eating nasty, toxic worms.
> The hunter rarely gives it chase: its meat
> Is not a dish he'd ever choose to eat.

The Old Testament included the stork among the unclean creatures and forbade the consumption of its flesh. It can be said, then, that nature conservation began centuries before our own age, when Yahweh instructed the children of Israel: 'And these are they which ye shall have in abomination among the fowls; they shall not be eaten, they are an abomination: the eagle, and the ossifrage, and the osprey, And the vulture, and the kite after his kind; Every raven after his kind; And the owl, and the night hawk, and the cuckow, and the hawk after his kind, And the little owl, and the cormorant, and the great owl, And the swan, and the pelican, and the gier eagle, And the stork, the heron after her kind, and the lapwing, and the bat.'

The stork didn't find its way onto the dinner table, but it did fall victim to folk medicine. Janota notes that the innards of the bird were 'a treatment for colic and inflammation of the kidneys', its fat 'was rubbed on limbs stricken with gout or the shivering fit', while its heart 'boiled in water and taken with that water, is prescribed for epilepsy'. For health purposes the foul meat was eaten too: 'Even [Italian naturalist, Ulisse] Aldrovandi considered it effective for palsy and strokes.'

The bile was prescribed for aching eyes, while the stomach ('dried and ground') helped with food poisoning. Even stork droppings were swallowed, dissolved in water. 'In the Sudeten Foothills, in the 1890s a case was recorded of parts of the wattle from a stork's nest (consisting of a mixture of excrement and mud) being gathered, with the intention of feeding it to a child suffering from epilepsy.' The administration of that cure seems to have been prevented.

In Greece, after the Turkish yoke was cast off, storks were almost wiped out, because the occupiers had treated them with solicitude. Luckily the population survived. At their African wintering grounds, the birds are still hunted for their meat. In 1822 in Klütz in Mecklenburg a stork was shot and stuffed that had a decorated arrowhead protruding from its body. It can be seen today in the museum of the University of Rostock. Hunting methods have not radically changed in the past 200 years. Some time ago near Bełchatów a stork appeared with an arrow stuck in its leg. The wound had healed cleanly, and the bird had learned to live with a sharp object sticking out of its limb.

I reach another village along a potholed road; on the horizon a gigantic thunderhead is already looming. An apocalyptic downpour is on the cards. The nest can be seen from far off, but the storks aren't in it. The first person I meet gives me all the information I need: three young reared successfully, one thrown out that lived and is being looked after by the owners of the house. I see the stork squatting on its still-black young legs, next to a tan mongrel lying on its back. An elderly gentleman says that the bird belongs to his son, who took it in and raised it. The stork would probably have been grateful if it had known what gratitude is, but according to Polish law the son isn't allowed to keep it as a mascot. I keep my thoughts to myself.

Chicks and eggs thrown out of storks' nests were, depending on the region, a sign of a good harvest or a bad one, rain or drought. Farmers, subject to the vagaries of weather, would look everywhere for signs. And storks raised by humans were a permanent feature of the rural landscape. All those Wojteks, Kajteks, Kubas. Maria Kownacka's *Adventures of Kajtek* concerns just such a stork raised on a farm. The indispensable Janota reports that a certain veterinarian of Flensburg by the name of Hanson 'recommended that each year one young stork be taken from each nest, raised through the winter then, after its wings are clipped, that it be used for mousing'.

A considerable part of the life of Władysław Aleksander Malecki is a mystery. We know that this forgotten landscapist of the late nineteenth century graduated from the School of Fine Arts in Warsaw. He supposedly took part in the January Uprising of 1863–64, though it hasn't been possible to confirm the stories passed down in his family. Later, like many Polish artists of the period, he lived for a long while in Munich. His painting was heavily influenced by the Barbizon School (especially Constant Troyon), which called on painters to quit the city and return to the pure *paysage*. Another artist Malecki held in high esteem was Courbet, participant in the Paris Commune and uncompromising realist, who in 1866 had painted a picture of a vagina and titled it brazenly *The Origin of the World*.

Malecki himself, though, was no scandalmonger. He was interested in unalloyed landscape; in his paintings humans are no more than a fleck of colour designed to enliven the canvas. In 1874 he painted his best known work: *The Storks' Parliament*. The birds are preparing to depart. The mature, dark greenery of August is dimming as the sun sets. The white storks contrast with the sombre background of the trees. A stream, and gloomy trunks along its banks. Poplars? Willows? My expert claims that birches growing by a marsh can be that dark. The weekly *Tygodnik Illustrowany* wrote that the painting 'is so full of charm that one is almost incapable of turning one's eyes away'. The melancholy of summer's end. Malecki's life at that time was painted in similarly darkening colours. The impoverished artist was taken in by the mayor of Szydłowiec, who let him live in the tower of the town hall. Malecki painted the town, its views, its major buildings. Things went badly for him. Unimaginably badly. He died of hunger and exhaustion in 1900.

It starts to rain so heavily that I can't see the road in front of me. I cling to the shoulder and hope I won't be hit by some distracted tractor driver. The temperature drops, the windows steam up. A wind stirs, then a moment later the trumpets of the apocalypse fall silent. Luckily summer showers are short-lived. In Strzyżyn I see a platform on a pole, but the houseowner explains that it's been waiting for storks for a dozen years or more. From time to time they come by, stand up there and scan the neighbourhood, but nothing comes of it. Maybe because the platform, which is made from a plastic table-top, bows slightly beneath their weight? Storks typically avoid such an unstable base. 'Storks are poor builders and their nests are carelessly constructed, but for all that, they're as strong and sturdy as peasant cottages,' wrote the naturalist, educationalist and folklorist Mieczysław Brzeziński.

In less than a month the gatherings will begin. They're called 'sejmiki' – diets, or little parliaments – in Polish. At one time it was believed that the storks gather in flocks to try any bird guilty of marital infidelity. A second item on the agenda was supposedly a flying exam for young birds. Towards the end of August the storks set off together for Africa. They travel dozens, even hundreds of miles per day. Everything depends on the weather – storks mostly fly by gliding, so they need warm, rising currents of air. This is possible only between ten in the morning and four in the afternoon, when the earth is sufficiently warmed up. Storks spend almost four months out of the year on their migration. Now, at the end of July, the young are not yet ready to set off for the wintering grounds.

Every year fewer of them return. Poland is no longer the main haven for storks; more of them stay in Spain. In the Opole region in the south-west the population has dropped more than 40 per cent in only a decade. There are many causes: pesticides, monoculture, drainage and the forestation of unused land. In my district here things aren't quite so bad. At its very edge, in the village of Augustów, only one nest is left, with a single young stork. In June there were two; but some other storks came by, there was a fight, and one chick died. An older guy lying on a pile of planks asks indignantly: 'Look, why were there always three or four of them and now, f—k it, there's only the one?'

TWO HOURS
OF DAYLIGHT LEFT

WHEN YOU AGREE TO MEET up with someone in the middle of the night you're guaranteed slippage of three quarters of an hour, but we're one-and-a-half hours late from the start. I slept less than an hour, but we're buoyed up by excitement and the promise of something exotic (in Polish terms), so we do a good job of making up for lost time. The last sixty miles, though, don't go as fast as they could. Here a cigarette by a ruined larchwood manor, there fries at McDonald's, and buying supplies too. Then right near the end we get a bit lost. We arrive in the early afternoon. In the mountains there's a lot of snow, and we don't have tyre chains or a tow rope. For the moment the wheels turn smoothly in the melting white mush; when it gets dark, the mush will turn to ice.

Lorries are coming downhill loaded with lumber – Carpathian spruce and beech. There's the sound of chain saws, warning signs, deep ruts left by logs that were hauled down the mountainside. At a turning there's a lumber shed, with a vintage Ural truck parked alongside. I rode in a big monster like that once in Chornohora in Ukraine; the young woodsman who drove it had lined the entire cabin with Turkish chewing gum stickers. It stank of gasoline and shook like a tank. Funny coincidence, because we're here for another Ural – the Ural owl.

It often hunts by day, spending the night in holes and crevices of splintered beech trees. At its nest it can be very aggressive; it won't hesitate to attack a human. Ringers wear ice-hockey masks when they climb up to find young Ural owls. I remember seeing photographs of an Estonian ornithologist's bleeding back, torn by owl talons. 'It demonstrates great attachment to its offspring; after the loss of an egg or a chick it howls mournfully and leaves that inhospitable place for many years,' writes Władysław Taczanowski in *Birds of Poland*. In the hooting of the Ural owl, he goes on, 'Siberians detect a resemblance to the word *shuba*, or fur coat, and they say that this bird, when it draws close to the habitations of humans in the autumn, constantly reminds them to wrap up warmly for the winter.'

It seems this large bird likes to perch by the road along which the lumber trucks pass. Some keen birders I know spent three days patrolling it, driving back and forth and barely getting out of their car. It's a lovely road – the old spruces on the north side are covered with caps of snow. But after two hours we know every tree. Twice we accidentally stray off the roadway, and each time we're towed out of the ditch by amused locals. I want to see the Ural owl, M. wants to photograph it, and we haven't driven 300 miles to stare through the car window at a wall of trees.

They began their ascent of the mountainside one afternoon in late December 1994: Jean-Marie Chauvet, an archaeologist with a bent for speleology, and two friends of his, Éliette Brunel and Christian Hillaire. The researcher's attention had earlier been drawn to a small crevasse in a rock face right next to a popular trail in the Ardèche Valley. A waft of air coming from the gap suggested that behind the rock debris there was a cave. The three cavers set about moving the boulders aside, and soon they revealed a small opening that led them to the rim of a shaft in the rock. They took their specialist equipment from their car and entered the cave.

They found two huge chambers whose walls glittered from the minerals embedded in them. Formations of calcite and other concretions that had developed over thousands of years hung from the ceiling; the ground was littered with bones of cave bears and ibexes. On one of the stalactites Brunel noticed a small image of a mammoth painted in ochre. The three friends set about combing the cave, and they soon discovered more prehistoric artwork. There were drawings depicting creatures that had been extinct for millennia: lions and cave bears, woolly rhinoceroses, and also wild horses and bison. Later research revealed that the paintings were among the oldest in Europe, having been executed around 30,000 BCE.

The cave artists were masters of their craft; the pictures show that many of them understood and used foreshortening. The fighting rhinoceroses, drawn in charcoal, are depicted in dynamic poses. The studies of horse and lion profiles are vivid and strikingly realistic. The running bison have multiple legs – a kind of early animation suggesting a sequence of movements. Perhaps by the pale light of a torch the animals came to life before the eyes of the cave people? The paintings discovered by

Chauvet have none of the primitivism or lack of skill that might be expected of Palaeolithic art.

In the morning we're back on the same old road, but we promise one another we won't waste the entire day like this. In the spruces two inquisitive nutcrackers with black beaks are flitting about. Here they're timid and don't let themselves be approached, whereas at Morskie Oko Lake in the Tatras their kinsmen hop unceremoniously onto the picnic tables outside the shelter. We walk up to a small clearing. In the snow there are traces of feet and wings. Was the Ural owl hunting here? I take a photo – maybe someone will confirm it. A pair of ravens fly overhead and as if on command plummet down simultaneously with folded wings. One bird croaks hoarsely, the other makes a noise that sounds like a stick rattling against bicycle spokes. Clonk, clonk. In the wood I jump over a dip and sink to my knees in a puddle hidden under the snow. Water seeps over the top of my boots.

We go back to our accommodation, eat something, I change and we're back on that damn road. The last time, we swear. The daylight is diminishing. We drive slowly and I notice a bird with its back to us in the brush. It's amazing how many impulses can speed through your brain in a single instant. I see brown feathers through my binoculars, I think at once, 'owl', and almost at the same moment I reject the idea. No, it's not the Ural owl. The bird turns in profile: it's a female hazel grouse, perching on the slim bowed branches of a small tree. Its looks about uneasily, and when M. gets out with his camera it drops lower in a flutter of wings. M. says that earlier on he heard the chirping sound of the hazel grouse, which sounds more like a small passerine.

Soon after, a woodpecker crosses our path in a deep sinusoidal flight. In an old wood like this, with lots of rotting timber, there may well be something of interest. A female white-backed woodpecker with the distinctive barring on its chest peeks out from behind a branch (in the morning I was almost certain I heard its tell-tale slow drumroll). The situation repeats: M. gets out with his gear, the bird starts up and disappears among the trees. M. apologises for scaring it away, but I don't mind; I saw the bird only briefly, but it was a clear and relatively close sighting. A photographer needs more time to get the most out of his model. Rarely satisfied with a single shot, he's likely to keep taking pictures as long as the bird allows it. M. hadn't even had time to lift the camera to his eye.

We have two more hours of daylight left (I'm starting to talk like M.), and we set off for a valley we found on the map. The river here constitutes the border; in the distance we can hear the barking of a Ukrainian dog. Across the water, modest green cottages cluster together in the cold. A snow-covered field is flooded with the pink light of the setting sun. A couple of hundred metres from the car I spot a motionless fox. It stares at us, its head between its black paws. M. gets out, but the fox quickly turns around, shows us its beautiful bushy tail, and in a couple of bounds it's in a rut made by a border patrol snowmobile. It scuttles off towards Ukraine. Animals often watch the car curiously; usually, after a moment, they go back to what they were doing, but when people start to get out they scarper.

In one of the cave's chambers, images made with a different technique were found. The limestone in this part of the cave is covered with a layer of clay, and the Palaeolithic artist was equally capable of utilising this material. Next to the mammoths and horses gouged into the wall is the first-known image of a bird. The coating of clay must have been thick and soft in this place, since the picture was made with a finger. A prehistoric owl is shown from behind (you can tell from the way the wings are folded), but its head with two tufts of feathers is turned to the viewer. The minimalism of the representation gives it an air of mystery.

On the official webpage for the cave we read that it's a long-eared owl. But that delicate, usually woodland owl doesn't really belong in a rock cliff. For this reason some specialists claim that the prehistoric drawing shows an eagle owl. Both species have feathery 'ears' on the top of their head, though they're very different in size. The artist did not reproduce the bird exactly, of course – no doubt he observed it from a considerable distance. But it's certain that many generations of eagle owls perched at the entrance to the Chauvet cave.

Images of owls have been found in other caves too. Why were they of particular interest to our ancestors? The Trois Frères cave in the Pyrenees boasts a family portrait of snowy owls, made almost 20,000 years ago. An adult bird and two chicken-like young, gouged into the wall. They're looking directly at us. In fact, owls are usually shown face on. Perhaps because their large eyes, like ours, are forward-facing? Is that what gives the birds their metaphysical profundity? Also striking is their flat 'face' of feathers around the beak and eyes – the so-called facial disk. Owls seen in profile do not make such an unsettling impression.

Slowly we drive back. As we climb another incline from the hollow of a stream, in the branches of a willow I catch a glimpse of a burly, unmistakable form. I've never seen a Ural owl before, but I needed only a split second to be absolutely sure. 'Pull over,' I say as calmly as I can. I'm afraid that too much excitement will land us in the ditch again, and here, close to the border, there's very little traffic, and no one's around to pull us out. 'What is it?' asks M. 'Back up a couple of metres – on your side there's a Ural in a willow,' I explain in a level voice. We roll back downhill. The owl is perching with its back to us, but for a moment it turns its extraordinary face towards us. The Ural is strong, with a long tail, and it looks twice as big as an ordinary tawny owl. After a moment it turns to the meadow again and goes back to listening.

A Ural owl can hear its prey under a fifty-centimetre layer of snow. Its large head, bending down intently, looks rather comical. The frost has begun to kick in again, and the heavy snow, warmed in the sun, covers over once more with a coating of crisp ice that crunches underfoot. There's no way of sneaking up on the bird. It moves to a further tree. Maybe the sound of the turn indicator disturbed it? It makes a deep wing-beat, then like a hawk glides soundlessly out over the meadow. It perches on a hayrick like a buzzard. M. gets in a few shots, though the sun dropped behind the mountains some time ago. The photographs look pretty good, but the owl has its back to us in most of them. M. is unhappy: 'If only we'd seen it ten minutes earlier!' Me, I have nothing to complain about: the woodpecker, the hazel grouse, the owl – a good tally.

M. always needs more time than I do, and the right conditions, but even when he has them he's rarely satisfied. For the rest of the day he harps on about the missed chance. As we're going back in the gathering gloom, just outside the village, on the slender skeleton of an aspen we see a massive ball with a long tail – another Ural. Its silhouette stands out clearly against the fading horizon. It's already too dark for a decent photograph. The owl rises from its branch and disappears amid the trees along the river. Its grey plumage is entirely invisible in the dusk.

Perhaps it's because of the facial disk, that feather face with its watchful features, that we ascribe intelligence to the owl? After all, it was the symbol of Athena, the goddess of wisdom. Did the ancient Greeks have a particular species in mind? Biologists have identified it as the little owl, giving it the Latin name *Athene noctua*. In reality owls are neither exceptionally intelligent nor particularly cunning, and their striking appearance is the result of adaptation to living in darkness. The large head conceals amazingly sensitive ears beneath its plumage, and the radially arranged feathers of the facial disk act as a kind of dish antenna in gathering sounds. The large, wise eyes capture as much light as possible from the surroundings, to enable the bird to hunt at night.

The following day a Ural owl, which weighs around one kilogram, is sitting on the crown of a spruce. Right at the dangerously curving tip. It's handsome in the rays of the timid morning sun. Its light-grey feathers with dark shafts, the circular facial disk; and its eyes, black like those of a tawny owl, looking at us languidly and indifferently. M. leans out of the car, manages a few shots, but then the owl flies off. M. checks the screen of his camera and is furious again – he pulled over two metres too soon. The pictures are spoiled by a horizontal branch in the foreground that cuts the bird in two. The light was ideal. But, who knows, if we'd driven two more metres forward maybe he wouldn't even have had time to take out the camera?

Birdwatchers often resent photographers. It's a long-running dispute over ethics. Is it acceptable to approach closer if the bird feels threatened? The low cost and wide availability of equipment have made it seem as though anyone can become a photographer, regardless of whether they know how to take pictures. The internet is chock-a-block with mediocre photographs whose only value lies in the fact that they show every detail of a bird's plumage. M. is technically skilled, he knows exactly what effect he wants to achieve, and he has something else that money can't buy: talent. He's able to suppress his instincts and stop at a considerable distance if he determines that taking one more step is redundant. Despite that, the birds often fly away when they see a lens aimed at them.

The owl drops into a willow and goes back to its hunting. Ural owls hunt from a perch; they listen closely and swoop down on the place where they hear a sound. Yet they also sometimes carry out recce flights like a harrier. Our bird flies in a low circle over the meadow on its long, rounded wings. When it sees or hears a movement it attacks, digging its talons into the snow. We drive past a barrier bearing a *Stop* sign. M. tries to turn around, but one front wheel slides into the snow-filled ditch. We struggle with the car for half an hour. It digs ever deeper into the snow, and we're losing out on the best light. It's Sunday; all day we've only seen one car on the road along the border, so we're going to have to walk the mile and a half or so to the village to see if someone can come out with a tractor.

We're lucky again – we stop a local kid in a Nissan four-wheel drive. He has a good pair of binoculars around his neck, and he's also looking for birds. 'Don't go beyond the barrier or they'll slap a damn fine on you.' This is deer-hunting season and there are hunters around; foresters don't mess about. The four-wheel dances a bit on the ice but it pulls our car out of the ditch. I'm now seeing things entirely through M.'s eyes. The sun has turned into a cloudy light bulb; for two hours it'll be too bright to take photographs. The Ural owl sits on a birch tree, we sit in the car. We're making sure it doesn't disappear – there's no point in bothering it now. We see it swoop down and strike softly but vigorously into the snow. It stays on the ground for a moment then flies up into a tree. This time it missed.

Even today the hooting of an owl makes people shudder uneasily. An atavistic fear of what lurks in the darkness connects us potently to our ancestors. In the black of night a soundless, demonic-looking creature is waiting. The oldest superstitions held that owls are emissaries of evil forces. In Slavic folklore the form of a tawny owl was taken by a woodland spirit called *lesavik* in Belarus, *leshy* in Russia, and in Poland *boruta* (it was only later that this spirit came to be identified with the Christian Devil). The Polish word *strzyga* – meaning the ghost of someone dead that persecutes the living – is a borrowing from the Latin *strix*, which in turn comes from the Greek *strinx*. *Strix aluco* is the Latin name of the tawny owl.

Sunday photographers know no moderation – they run around after birds completely mindlessly, not giving them a minute's peace and hampering their quest for food. Another problem is that of photographing birds in their nests, when they're feeding their young or incubating their eggs. If it's done in a clumsy, inexperienced way, the parent birds can become so alarmed that they abandon their young. Pictures of that kind should be the province of highly qualified, knowledgeable photographers. 'Despite the popular saying, the end does NOT justify the means... *primum non nocere*,' Dr Marek Keller reminds us in his article on birdwatching ethics. Yet we shouldn't exaggerate either. Snapping a picture of a great tit by its nesting box in a public park is not the same as photographing rare species of birds that are sensitive to human presence.

In birding circles everyone has heard some story or other about photographers unscrupulously taking pictures of rollers by their tree-hole nests. For a long time now rollers have been struggling to survive in Poland. Their population is very small. Scientists try to keep the location of nests a secret, but they don't always succeed. Photographers, dreaming of snapping these fabulously colourful birds, set up their equipment right by the nests, or they damage the habitat, for example removing branches that spoil their view. What happens afterwards to these images? You can't just show them around. To take photographs of rollers on their nests, you need special permission (and it's not granted to just anyone). What good comes of photographs taken by a vandal photographer? Does he frame them and hang them in his basement like a collector of stolen art? Does he bask in the beauty of the roller on his own, or in the company of trusted accomplices?

I heard another story about live chickens being tied by the leg to a stake so they couldn't escape from an approaching bird of prey. The photographer simply wanted the perfect picture of talons reaching out for their victim. In 2013 the Mazowsze region was visited by a hawk owl, a species that lives in the tundra and is rarely seen in Poland. The bird stopped in one place for quite some time, thus attracting birdwatchers from the entire country. Camera owners were especially interested in pictures of the hawk owl hunting; they bought mice in pet shops and enticed their sitter with them. An indication of degraded standards was the news that one photographer had tied a mouse to a piece of fishing line and was waving the creature at the end of a rod under the bird's nose. The owl put up with the interest shown in it (birds from the unpopulated far north are evidently more forbearing); it had more food than it needed, so in the end it began to warehouse mice in the gutter of a nearby house. In the end it flew away.

The Polish name of the little owl – *pójdźka* – comes from its ominous-sounding voice, which has traditionally been rendered as '*pójdź, pójdź w dołek pod kościołek*' – 'go, go down in the hole outside the church'. The scops owl in Antonello da Messina's Antwerp version of his *Crucifixion* is precisely an omen of approaching death. It sits at the feet of the suffering Christ and the thieves twisting in their agony, and it stares unmovingly at the viewer. Owls were also inseparable companions of witches and wizards. It was believed that various parts of their bodies had magical properties. Amulets were made of their talons; their eggs were said to cure alcoholism or enable night vision. An owl's heart placed on the breast of a sleeping woman supposedly made her reveal her secrets.

The shadows are lengthening and the snow is turning crimson by the light of the setting sun. The Ural owl is lurking in the gloom by a stream, almost completely invisible. It's on my side of the car, so M. and I wriggle across and swap places. He sticks his lens out of the window, and I drive in rubber boots through which I can barely feel the pedals. The owl is perched on top of a rotten tree stump. A few photographs through the branches. We drive down the hill a short way and M. shouts: 'Stop!' I don't stop; I think I'm depressing the brake, but we keep moving. The trees are in the way again. The owl flies off. M. mutters about the missed opportunity. 'What a picture that would have been!'

We drive on a while, then I run uphill to scan the edge of the wood. M. calls from down below: 'Is it there?' 'No!' I shout back, then at that moment I see a puffy silhouette on a spruce. The sun is dropping behind the mountain, and its rays shine blood red on the pale down of the owl's breast. 'It's here!' I call. M. rushes up with his five kilos of gear; by the time he reaches me he's out of breath. The bird has moved to a different tree, where it's sitting facing us. I can see the last rays of the sun playing across its head. There's still some light. M. sneaks closer. The Ural doesn't react as it looks down at something and listens. Through my binoculars I watch it glancing at M. from time to time. In the end it flies down onto the snow, grabs some small shape in its talons, and disappears.

Time to go home. We just need to change into dry clothes. Right as I'm standing there with my trousers down, another Ural owl flies past thirty or forty metres away. I'm feeling content already; we've seen at least three birds, marvelled at their hunting and their easy, graceful flight. The sun has dropped behind the mountains, it's turned cold again, but M. jumps up and hurries out onto the meadow, tripod in hand. I watch through the binoculars as the bent-over human creeps up, while the owl sits on a fencepost with its back to him. M. crosses the sloping meadow. I know he's selecting his background. Meanwhile the bird flies low over the frozen surface. The snow no longer creaks underfoot, but breaks with a crunching sound. I stand in the road and watch the owl, which is busy thinking about itself and its belly, hopping from post to post. It's circling. M. comes back only when all that's left of the daylight is a faint yellow glow on the horizon. He's pleased.

Anything that lived in the darkness was unclean. The nightjar – a nocturnal bird that in shape looks a little like a small falcon, a little like a cuckoo – also seemed demonic. In the eighteenth century the English scholar Gilbert White noted a folk superstition according to which nightjars would cut open the skin of cattle and lay flies' eggs inside. Throughout Europe we find the belief that the bird would steal milk from the udders of cows and goats. In both Polish and English it has the sobriquet of 'goatsucker' ('*kozodój*'), and in Latin too – *caprimulgus*. Nightjars were in fact found on pastureland, since they would catch in flight the flies that accompany farm animals. Goatsuckers have small bills, but to suit their way of hunting they can open them very wide. Hieronymus Bosch gave one of his monsters the features of this bird. In the part of *The Garden of Earthly Delights* devoted to hell, we see a half man, half nightjar that is devouring and excreting human figures.

A good photographer has infinite patience. I've always been impressed by stories of waiting for hours in a hide or under camouflage netting. Of peeing into bottles, of numb legs and frozen fingers. In the magazine *Polish Birds* Artur Tabor, one of the best photographers of birds in the country, described how he managed to get a daytime picture of an eagle owl. A fellow photographer had found the bird's nest and built a hide, but he had to travel away at short notice. He offered Tabor the opportunity to take pictures, but on one condition – that he should not leave the hiding place. Movement could scare away the owl, which was sitting in the nest with its young.

On the first night there was a rainstorm. The tarpaulin roof of the shelter filled with rainwater which, leaking onto the photographer's head, ran inside his shirt and gathered under his backside on the inflatable mattress from which the air had escaped.

> For a while I turned my camera on infrared and I saw the female – she was sheltering her chicks with her body, water dripping off her beak and wings. When thunder sounded and lightning flashed, she would close her eyes and flinch in fear. In the morning the owls were so wretchedly rain-sodden they were misery incarnate. I couldn't take any photographs because the lens had steamed up and I had to wait till it cleared... The following night was horribly cold; there was even a slight frost, which I felt most painfully in the lower part of my body, since I was sitting the entire time in a wet chair. By the morning I'd lost all feeling.

At dawn the female left to hunt; it was only now there was a chance for the picture he'd been dreaming of. A couple of hours later the mother bird returned. 'I look gingerly through the viewfinder and what I see is reward for all my suffering,' he writes. 'The standing female fills the frame; she's looking at me, and she's magnificent. I focus cautiously and make the first photograph. I've got it! After a few more the female enters the nest and sits down on the chicks.'

A couple of days later the owner of the hide came back and finally liberated the photographer:

> I had to learn to walk again. I'd been sitting for so long in one position, with my legs immobile in the marsh, that now they wouldn't obey me… My frozen backside was like a board, for a month I couldn't feel anything there. But I'd photographed an eagle owl during the day. For someone who doesn't know the story they're just ordinary pictures but for me – they're the photographs of a lifetime.

It's true, I wasn't blown away by the image itself. A nice enough picture that only becomes interesting with the photographer's note. I love this story for its heroism, and for its ethical dimension. A thoroughgoing professional risks his own health because the comfort of an animal (!) is the most important thing to him. And also that empathy-filled description of the female shielding her young from the rain. As a sad postscript to this story, let it be said that Artur Tabor died doing what he most loved. He perished in an accident while photographing birds in Mongolia.

I tell this story to highlight one other thing also. Photography requires concentration, precision and patience. To take a good picture you need to spend a great deal of time with the bird (I'm not referring here to a picture that's a one-off chance success). If only for this reason, it seems to me that photographers who watch birds know their behaviour much better than many ornithologists. M. put me to shame once on a trip we took together to the Knyszyński Woods in hopes of seeing a pygmy owl. We set off in a sizeable group, though there were only two photographers among us. One of our number located the owl in a pine wood only a few miles from the sign to 'Białystok', the largest city in north-eastern Poland. The bird was flying quite high over the crowns of the pines. The birders who were seeing the little creature for the first time watched it for a while (meaning ten minutes or so), then decided they were ready for fresh excitement.

The suggestion that we go looking for another pygmy owl whose hunting territory was half a mile or so away was received without enthusiasm. We trailed over there. The trees grew lower and we found ourselves in a marsh. The bird appeared almost at once. This individual was not remotely timid, perching right over our heads, but we were so busy looking for it in the treetops that we only noticed it when it was flying away. The photographers wanted to stay; the rest of the group, however, insisted on going to get something to eat, finding our accommodation and visiting other places. The birdwatchers had had their fill. M. was disconsolate. We'd driven 120 miles to glance at the pygmy owl and check it off our life list? Who's more sensitive here – the photographer, who's cavalier and sometimes scares birds away,

A Ural owl, pre hunt

yet can also appreciate watching them for hours on end; or the birdwatcher, who keeps a safe distance, but is satisfied with the briefest look?

AT THE END
OF THE WORLD

IN THE BARTOSZYCE DISTRICT ADMINISTRATIVE offices it's hard to get any information about F. Tischler. I don't know much myself either: only his last name, his initial, and the fact that in 1941 he watched birds in this region. Jan Sokołowski mentions him in his *Birds of the Polish Lands*. But was Mr F. a professional naturalist or merely a keen amateur? A woodsman? Hunter perhaps? In those days nature was often observed with a shotgun or hunting rifle in hand. Did he live in these parts? Or was he only passing through?

In East Prussia at that time it was almost possible to forget that the most destructive war in the history of humankind was in progress. The area around Bartenstein (Bartoszyce), under German rule for centuries, didn't have to deal with the tribulations of partisan activity. True, the inhabitants despatched their obligatory contingent of recruits, and sometimes certain items were not available, but each year they gathered the harvest without hindrance, and their quiet was undisturbed by the crash of artillery or the drone of aircraft engines.

Official documents concerning the region's residents are said to have disappeared already in the 1940s. Were they destroyed? Taken away? In Lidzbark Warmiński soldiers of the Red Army made bonfires of German books and threw the charred remains into the Łyna River. At the offices I obtain only a phone number for a forester in the village of Minty; he's on leave, apparently, but he may know something about the mystery ornithologist. And, in fact, Mr Paweł Ulaniuk recalls a small memorial somewhere in the neighbouring woods that says something about Tischler. He advises me to try the forestry headquarters.

Here I get another good lead: Antoni Stecki, the deputy head forester, shows me a picture of a rock with a memorial plaque and tells me how to find it. 'In memory of eminent ornithologist and naturalist Dr Friedrich Tischler, 2 June 1881– 29 January 1945, and his wife Rose Tischler, née Kowalski, 31 May 1884–29 January 1945. From ornithologists in Poland and in Germany.' In two languages, Polish and German. So he was a naturalist after all; there's that wife with the Polish last name, and the same mysterious date of death. A lot of information, and even more questions.

❦

Lusiny is reached by an atrocious pitted road of hexagonal concrete paving stones. Former collective farm buildings and dilapidated labourer quarters now provide shelter for the most hopeless cases from Bartoszyce. In the summer the weeds come in through the windows, it seems. In addition, there is an avenue of lime trees leading to the Tischlers' former manor house and a few brick-built houses that have seen better days. After the collective farm closed down, only those who for whatever reason were unable to move from this godforsaken place stayed behind.

Mrs Majkowska didn't wish to leave her parents, though she was assigned accomodation in a block of flats in nearby Kinkajmy. Now she has to ride several miles on her bicycle to the nearest shop. She can't say much about the Tischlers – her parents settled here in the fifties. Brygida, who used to live with the collective farm manager, would have known them, but like almost everyone from the Masurian region she ended up leaving for Germany. Mrs Majkowska recalls only a gravestone that stood where the plaque is now. And she remembers something else that she'd rather forget: soldiers working on the farm who got drunk one night, tipped the desiccated bodies out of their coffins and left them on the road.

On the ground floor of the Lusiny manor house there used to be a shop. Back then several families lived in the two-storey building, but over the course of time the place emptied and fell more and more into disrepair. It was saved from complete ruin by a local potentate who decided to move in himself. The renovations have been going on for several years; apparently the new owner is at odds with the conservator. The site is fenced off. The manor is a fair-sized if somewhat plain building with a new roof and dilapidated walls. The owner has an office in nearby Sędławki.

'It isn't possible to meet with the chairman.' When Mr Stanisław speaks of his boss he bows his head in respect and closes his eyes.

This dedicated worker is from around here. He remembers how, as a child, along with the other boys he would sneak into the Tischler family vault to look at the caskets lined with oak shavings (that was how bodies were preserved hereabouts) and the old dried-up corpses. He recalls a severed head lying about somewhere in the bushes. The vault was dismantled in the mid-seventies or so; he doesn't know what happened to the bodies. As for the manor, 'there's nothing to see in there'. After the war, for a time a local man who had married one of the former maids lived in the house. Perhaps he'd be able to tell me something?

Gerard Kałdyński was born in what is today the Kaliningrad Oblast. He looks at me doubtfully, not really understanding why I'm interested in all this. His older brother Arno left for Germany many years ago; of those who lived here back then he's the only one left. He doesn't remember much about the Tischler house – he was very small then. But even the scraps lodged in his memory are questionable. Mr Gerard claims that the owners' upright piano and grandfather clock remained in the rooms. Could such valuable objects have survived the passage of the Red Army?

I clamber up the door laid over the damaged steps, and I'm in the home of Friedrich and Rose. In the hallway there's a partition with glass panes that partially hides the crumbling stairs. The plaster has been entirely scraped off the walls; they would be utterly bare if it weren't for the remnants of some lovely panelling by the windows – the new owner has decided to spare it. In front of the house on the side of the avenue of limes, where there are now piles of sand and of rubble, there must have been a flower bed, perhaps a tree providing shade for the house. I walk gingerly upstairs so as not to scare away the nuthatch digging in the new ceiling beams. The place is empty. Near the outside door there are some old bottles. I take the smallest one.

I visit Marian Szymkiewicz, director of the Natural History Museum in Olsztyn, who was one of the initiators of the modest memorial at Lusiny. It's a sunny day; large slabs of snow fall noisily from the roof. Mr Marian offers me an unexpected gift: two articles about Tischler. A German text by Christoph Hinkelmann, and an issue of the museum's journal, *Natura: the Natural World of Warmia and Masuria*, which includes a piece by Eugeniusz Nowak titled 'Friedrich Tischler (1881–1945): Eminent Ornithologist of East Prussia'. Nowak writes in his introduction:

> I spent several years of my life in Masuria, where I directed a small research station. My job included research on birds, which brought me in contact with a man who, though long dead, became through the scientific publications he left behind my most important advisor and assistant. My special relationship with Friedrich Tischler is very personal, since I was the first naturalist to locate his grave.

The Prussian landed gentry were a bastion of conservative values. The Tischlers' views, which were considered liberal in their circles, were probably formed by family trauma. Their ancestors, devout Calvinists, fled to Prussia from Salzburg to escape religious persecution. They settled here in the early nineteenth century, and Lusiny (Losgehnen) became their family home.

Yet Friedrich's passion in life was certainly not politics. He grew up under the influence of his live-in tutor Carl Borowski, a keen hunter. From his earliest years he collected plants for his herbarium, and assiduously pinned insects in cases. He kept a *Vogelbuch*, a journal in which he noted his observations about bird habits, behaviour and song. He hunted, then used the birds he shot for scientific purposes. The first trophy in his collection was a black woodpecker.

The Tischlers placed great emphasis on their children's education; the family produced several noted scientists. It was no surprise, then, that at the Bartenstein grammar school Friedrich was top of the class, with bad marks only in gymnastics. Despite his interest in nature he opted for more practical, dependable studies in the law. Yet he had no intention of abandoning his passion. In 1905 he published his first scientific article, about flocks of starlings. The following year he brought out a piece about the birds of Lake Kinkajmy, whose shore is a few hundred metres from the Lusiny mansion. After he graduated, Tischler sought work in his native region, wanting to continue his exploration of its natural world.

In 1908 he obtained a position as legal adviser at the court in Lidzbark. He refused later offers of promotion that would have entailed moving to a bigger town. From Lidzbark it was only twenty or so kilometres to Lusiny, and he spent all his free time there. He wasn't the globetrotting sort; for his holidays he always went to the Rossitten Bird Observatory (now the Rybachy Biological Station) on the Curonian Spit. In 1914 his first book appeared: *Birds of East Prussia Province*. It received favourable reviews. In his introduction, Tischler encouraged ornithologists to collaborate with him and send in their sightings.

Meanwhile, Europe was at war. It was the greatest, cruellest, most tragic conflict ever, in the eyes of its contemporaries. From today's perspective, it was little more than a warm-up for events that would unfold two decades later. But killing had never seemed easier – soldiers choked on mustard gas, were burned by flamethrowers and blown to pieces by bombs and tank shells. In hospitals thousands died of dysentery and typhus.

From his 1918 article on the stock dove, it's hard to tell whether Tischler was deeply affected by the defeat of Prussia. Did he follow the majority of his countrymen in regarding the Treaty of Versailles as an injustice and a humiliation? He certainly did not succumb to nationalistic sentiments where science was concerned. As he worked on his magnum opus, the two-volume *Birds of East Prussia and Its Environs*, he drew on the observations of Włodzimierz Puchalski, a Polish naturalist, photographer and filmmaker who gave us the concept of 'bloodless hunting'.

Birds of East Prussia and Its Environs appeared in 1941 and was enthusiastically received in ornithological circles. The modest civil servant of Lidzbark was showered with honours: an honorary doctorate from the University of Königsberg, membership in the Kaiser Wilhelm Society for the Advancement of Science (today's Max Planck Society).

His publications, though, drew attention beyond the world of science. In 1942 Tischler spent a week in the Białowieża

Forest, which was the apple of the eye of Hermann Göring, Reich Master of the Hunt and commander-in-chief of the Luftwaffe. Tischler wrote that his stay 'has something of the romanticism of [German adventure novelist] Karl May, which the German forest service countenances with good humour'. If I understand it properly: Nazis as cowboys, the local residents as redskins. In this comparison was there room for May's noble hero, Winnetou? 'He was isolated from reality and allowed only to go birdwatching,' Nowak writes, but it also sounds as if Tischler did not particularly go looking for reality.

I'm bothered by Tischler's attitude to Nazism. In 1933 Hitler comes to power, and we know only that our ornithologist is at that time researching the appearance in Prussia of a tundra sub-species of the ringed plover. I ask Eugeniusz Nowak if in his view Tischler could have been a Nazi. 'He considered himself a German patriot, but he never gave cause to be thought a jingoist.' Such a view was corroborated by his nephew, with whom he was close – Wolfgang Tischler, an eminent ecologist and professor at the University of Kiel. It's certain that Friedrich was not a member of the NSDAP (he doesn't appear in the membership rolls). He was, rather, politically naive. A typical introverted researcher devoted entirely to his preoccupation.

In his book *Scientists in the Hardest of Times*, Eugeniusz Nowak recounts the lives of naturalists, primarily ornithologists, who in various ways were affected by twentieth-century totalitarian regimes. Most of them were apolitical and turned to science as a haven, an escape from brutal reality. Not all succeeded. Some were assigned the historical role of victims, others became perpetrators or their accomplices. What is most striking, though, is the profound supranational, supra-ideological bond of brotherhood, confirmed by successive biographies, that links scientists in wartime.

It's hard to condemn Professor Erwin Stresemann who, it's true, was filled with pride when he read about the military triumphs of the Third Reich, yet who at the same time did not forget about his friends being held in POW camps.

To two British officers, John Buxton and George Waterston, he sent articles on ornithology, and rings so they could conduct research on the swallows that lived in their camp. His friend Günther Niethammer, on the other hand, one of the most eminent of German ornithologists, played his part as a perpetrator entirely convincingly. He joined the Waffen SS and served as a guard in Auschwitz. It sounds like a black joke, but even there, in the factory of death, he found time for birding. In 1942 he published 'Observations on the Birds of Auschwitz'. In a letter to Stresemann he boasted that he was a kind of 'master of the hunt' in the camp: he rode around on a bicycle with a shotgun, bagging animals (he had special permission to take away his kill). In the late 1960s Eugeniusz Nowak spoke with Dr Andrzej Zaorski, who immediately after the war had worked to save the surviving prisoners of Auschwitz. Zaorski had been amazed by the numerous bird boxes in the part of the camp where the personnel lived. In the commandant's safe he found Niethammer's article on the birds of Auschwitz, with a dedication to the commandant himself, Rudolf Höss. Several accounts testify to the fact that Niethammer was deeply affected by his time at Auschwitz, but his reputation as 'camp master of the hunt' was not improved by efforts after the war to hush up this inglorious part of his biography.

Nobel Prizewinner Konrad Lorenz also fell for national-socialist ideology. A born storyteller and author of enchanting books about geese and ravens, in wartime Poznań he worked on research that aimed at proving the superiority of the Aryan race. In the course of time he came to understand the criminality of the system he had served. From his later declarations and his conversations with Eugeniusz Nowak it appears that his conversion was sincere.

Nowak's book also includes a chapter on Friedrich Tischler.

Buxton and Waterston had colleagues in the POW camp, John Barrett and Peter Conder, who ringed birds with them. The quartet are the subjects of a very funny and very British book titled *Birds in a Cage*, by Derek Niemann. Niemann tells the story of these four officers and ornithologists who came to the conclusion that being in captivity was no reason to stop conducting scientific research. Yes, there's a war on, but birdwatching is always possible. The book's epigraph is by A.W. Boyd, who in September 1939 wrote in his weekly column: 'I cannot help thinking that if only Hitler had been an ornithologist, he would have put off the war until the autumn migration was over.'

The British officers conducted their observations in a very methodical manner. During a special mission to the Norwegian fjords, Buxton noted the early migration of the swallow, while Waterston, who was assigned to the defence of the airport at Maleme in Crete, recorded a woodchat shrike in his notebook. Captivity changed little. The prisoners complained only about their lack of freedom to move about the terrain (the fence!), and that in order to inspect the nests inside the camp they weren't allowed to simply borrow a ladder. They researched the breeding habits of common species; they peered over the barbed wire and carefully noted the numbers of birds passing through in the autumn.

All four survived the war. While still in the camp John Buxton had begun his observations of the habits of the common redstart, which later became the subject of his book *The Redstart*, regarded as a masterpiece of ornithological writing. George Waterston established a research centre on Fair Isle in the Shetlands, and popularised nature tourism. John Barrett wrote a guide to sea birds that for decades was the most widely used book of its kind. Peter Conder became president of the Royal Society for the Protection of Birds, which he transformed into an influential organisation with hundreds of thousands of members.

Lusiny, a year before the war. Friedrich Tischler leans back against a doorway onto a broad veranda. In the background there's a wicker armchair. He's looking at the camera. His features are stern, he's squinting. No wonder – he has the sun in his eyes. Is that why he looks a little impatient? Or perhaps someone dragged him away from his work? That would be suggested by the open drill jacket. Under it he wears a white shirt with a wing collar. He's on the slender side, bald, and in his wire-rimmed glasses he looks like a pastor. Binoculars hang from his neck. They're probably Zeiss 8 x 30s, perfect for birdwatching in the woods.

The winter of 1944–45. The outcome of the war is a foregone conclusion. The Thousand-Year Reich is doomed. The more far-sighted inhabitants of East Prussia don't wait around for the Soviet soldiers to come knocking at their door. They pack up their belongings and flee westward. Meanwhile, Friedrich Tischler takes melancholic walks around his property. Every now and then he stops, raises his binoculars to his eyes, notes something down. Waxwings, crossbills, bullfinches. Passing flocks of twite land for a moment in the fields. There are interesting birds to watch in any season.

In the past year he's published two articles, one about the black-eared wheatear in Latvia, the other about the first confirmed three-toed woodpecker in East Prussia. Tischler isn't interested in the situation at the front; perhaps he thinks that such things do not concern him. He's working on a third volume of *Birds of East Prussia and Its Environs*, unaware that any moment now East Prussia will cease to exist. In mid-January 1945 he writes to his nephew Wolfgang Tischler: 'We're doing fine here. We're calmly waiting for the new [German] offensive.'

How very naive he was! Eugeniusz Nowak thinks Friedrich must have been swayed by the intensified propaganda campaign ordered by Erich Koch, the Gauleiter of the region. Tischler probably could not conceive of a German defeat, or imagine that even his Lusiny homeland would be affected by the war. But less than two weeks later the Red Army was a stone's throw away. Walter von Sanden, a naturalist from the Warmia region, tried to make it through to Tischler as he fled on his bicycle from his family estate at Guja, but he was blocked by the line of the front.

On 23 January 1945 Friedrich Tischler sent a postcard to his relatives in Kiel, telling them that at the moment the Red Army entered his native village he and his wife would commit suicide. The card might come in useful later in dealing with the inheritance. At the last moment a man called Mithalter from a place called Mackow tries to persuade him to leave. Tischler thanks him for his concern, but refuses. He stands by the steps leading to the veranda with binoculars in hand, watching some birds that are hidden in the treetops. What was he looking at in late January 1945? Perhaps at the nuthatches that still trill today in the lime tree avenue leading to the manor?

Tischler's nephew Wolfgang learned of the circumstances surrounding the death of the ornithologist and his wife from their coachman Karol Hartwig. A doctor friend of theirs provided the poison. Hartwig was ordered to dig a grave; evidently they did not wish to rest in the family vault. Nowak believes that the couple killed themselves on the evening of 29 January; Hinkelmann thinks it was more likely to have been the 31st. Rose fell by the vault, Friedrich at the edge of the freshly dug grave. Was such a drastic step called for? When in 1962 Eugeniusz Nowak spoke with a local Masurian woman who had witnessed the Red Army entering the village, he was told that they didn't spare anyone. All the men regardless of age were shot, and 'their bodies lay scattered in the snow for several days'.

Lusiny. An elderly man sitting in front of the house says that last year some Germans were here. They were interested in the graves by the manor pond. What graves? He doesn't know, and I can't remember seeing anything around the manor that looked like a cemetery. The 'pond' is more of a rubble-filled pool that hasn't yet dried up after the spring rains. Maybe that was where they buried the locals who were shot in January 1945?

If you squint, from the windows of the Tischler residence you can see the country house at Glitajny on a nearby rise. Its owner, Georg Bormann, fled from the Red Army in the night of 28 to 29 January. We don't know if he contacted his neighbours. The two places are separated by a narrow marshy valley. The house at Glitajny is still in pretty good shape – its handsome laurel-leaf stucco work is intact. The Tischler's home was much less impressive. I meet a local beekeeper who after the war lived there with his family. 'The place was full of life!' he says.

Eugeniusz Nowak writes in an email that, when he visited Lusiny in the 1960s, he saw the mummified body of one of the Tischler ancestors that had been dragged out of its tomb. Along with a collective farm worker and two locals he put it back in its coffin. Devastated by such desecration, he never wrote about the incident. But he reported it to the head of the

A kingfisher on the move

regional Home Affairs Department in Olsztyn. The official admitted that 'it wasn't the first time something like that had happened', and the two of them concluded that it would be best to bury the bodies in the ground and to dismantle the vault, which was vulnerable to attack by local louts.

From what I've been able to ascertain, the structure stood in the Lusiny woods for at least another decade. Even today, in the springtime, when the undergrowth isn't too high the outline of the foundations can be made out. Shards of red roof tiles lie scattered. In the sixties you could still see the rounded top of the grave in which Friedrich and Rose's bodies were probably placed. Afterwards, the Tischlers' resting place was swallowed up by the woods. Thanks to the efforts of Eugeniusz Nowak and Marian Szymkiewicz, a small boulder with a memorial plaque was put up here towards the end of the 1990s.

On Lake Kinkajmy, a couple of hundred metres from the memorial stone, a light rain is falling. Kinkeimer See – the name appears many a time in Tischler's articles. The damp drizzle sticks to the body. Cranes pace slowly across a stubble field. A drab youngster sits down on the ground under the watchful eye of the adults. The bright blue wing of a kingfisher flashes along a narrow channel cut out of the vegetation. On the shore an angler sits motionless, enveloped in a rain cape; behind a screen of reeds are pale herons that are equally immobile. Silence. Only the swallows are twittering harmoniously over the surface of the water.

CLAYPIT PARK

IF I WERE A BIRD, the field guide would say of me that I 'lead an exceptionally sedentary existence'. I've lived in the same place all my life. For more than thirty years I've observed every summer, autumn, winter and spring in Szczęśliwice: the first frost, first snow, first white blossoms on the cherry tree by my apartment block. I'm a bit like a sparrow, which rarely goes outside its immediate neighbourhood. What that neighbourhood looks like I couldn't say – I'm not able to see it through someone else's eyes. I think it's pretty quiet – only very occasionally a football fan yells 'Legiaaa!' in the middle of the night like a wounded animal, or smashes up a bench. Residential blocks from the 1970s, a large housing estate, grey buildings covered with an apricot-coloured frosting of Styrofoam. Luckily the smog and the lichen have given it a bit of a patina. But the most precious thing is the park.

➤

It arose out of uncultivated fields, the remnants of suburban orchards, and trash heaps. Meadows where Roma would camp. Old brickmaking clay pits now filled with water. For that reason there are no ancient trees here, or spectacular classical architecture. The park's lineage is plebeian. A small hill formed on a base of rubbish, tangles of old rags, scrap metal and bricks left over from the uprising of 1944. 'A rubbish dump formed there and kept growing, like a lunar mountain chain. The trash smoked and burned; at times, in the night there was a glow as if from a mighty conflagration,' Marek Nowakowski wrote of post-war Szczęśliwicki. Subcutaneous shifts here are constantly pushing mysterious rods and cables up out of the ground.

The uneven steppe with its clay-pit ponds was civilised towards the end of the 1960s. Two lakes were joined with a canal, the hill was given a more regular shape. The new Szczęśliwicki Park was planted with poplars, short-lived over-achievers that are the first to shoot up in the race for sunlight. Willows bowed their heavy, shaggy heads over the banks of the clay pit. A pine wood was planted, which now serves as a makeshift toilet. As late as the early 1990s the hill was encircled on the south side by fallow fields and cabbage patches. Startled pheasants would clatter up from the brush. It's a quiet place with rocky soil, not entirely safe, with a dusty road leading to the train tracks. Somewhere in there we buried my first dog, but his remains were not able to rest in peace. Change came thundering in.

The 1990s performed unsuccessful plastic surgery on the neighbourhood. A forest of cranes sprang up around the park, menacing the hill with their long arms. Cramped plasterboard housing estates, which looked as though they'd been grafted from some cheap Mediterranean resort, spread throughout the area. A church popped up on the outskirts of the park, taking advantage of the favourable political climate. And on the hill itself a monument to our times was constructed – an All-Year

Ski Slope. The summit was elevated, the sides smoothed out and covered with white bristles resembling snow. A fence was put up. But the expected crowds never materialised. How was it possible that skiers didn't turn their backs on the Tatras and the Austrian Alps and rush over to slalom their way down our magnificent hill? There's also a swimming pool, open three months in the year. There are three exercise areas, three playgrounds, two soccer fields, two courts for volleyball and one for basketball, a tennis net and a café. More investments are on their way. How much park is left in the park?

An overcast winter daybreak enwrapped in fog. Dozens of gulls sit in the stillness. The majority of them are black-headed gulls, with the dark crescent behind the eye; among them are a few common gulls. In Polish their name was changed from 'common gull' to 'grey gull', because how can you protect a bird whose population by definition ought not to be a cause for concern? The gulls spend the night on the ice-covered clay-pit pond, unmoving and alert. Around eight they disperse noisily among the neighbouring residential blocks. They visit the rubbish skips, check out squares they know. There they'll always find some bread lying around – white, dark, or green with mould. Fresh, dry, rock-hard.

Nothing escapes their attention. They tirelessly harry some other birds that have found some old soup bones somewhere. They chase them till they make the lucky finders drop their booty. Interestingly, when a gull is captured, its first instinct is to regurgitate everything it ate most recently – for what could its oppressors be after if not food? When it turns really cold, brawny herring gulls and Caspian gulls visit the park. There's never more than a dozen of them, though. They're more distrustful, wary. It takes more energy and more time to lift such a large body off the ground, so these giants take no chances, they keep their distance from humans. They don't jostle for the food thrown down at the edge of the pond.

Up till the point when ice covers the surface of the water, the bank is patrolled by secretive moorhens. The moment they see a person, they scuttle behind the palisade of dry reeds. In the winter silence it's sometimes possible to hear the subdued metallic whistle of bullfinches, whose stocky figure was studied by Albrecht Dürer. On a massive forsythia bush hundreds of sparrows are chirping; in the early morning they look like tiny feathered baubles. Life gathers now around the feeders. Woodpeckers hang from openings in plastic bottles; below them, tree sparrows peck at the seed they scatter. It's only in late February that things start to happen. The tits chirrup more cheerfully, the crows set about refurbishing their nests. One pair I've got to know watch as I brush my dog. I throw away the bits of fluff, and one of the crows pursues them across the grass. It gathers whatever it can, while it can. With a beak full of dog hair it looks as though it's grown a big ruddy moustache. Like the young Kaiser Franz Joseph.

Photographers from all over Warsaw were chasing after them: a pair of Syrian woodpeckers, now called 'white-necked woodpeckers' in Polish, were the stars of Szczęśliwice. Their name is not a misnomer – the species really does come from Asia Minor; then in the early nineteenth century they expanded into the Balkans. Year by year, successive populations have moved north. The first Syrian woodpeckers hatched their chicks in a Polish tree hole towards the end of the seventies. They were especially drawn to city parks, in particular old fruit trees there. They're also fond of the soft wood of willows and poplars. Their exotic origins aren't immediately apparent; in fact, they're remarkably similar to great spotted woodpeckers, with whom in addition they can interbreed.

What tells them apart? Details. The Syrian didn't become the white-necked woodpecker for nothing. The 'moustache' on its cheek doesn't join at the back, so the neck is entirely white, the under-tail coverts pink, not livid red like its relative's, and the end of the tail is black with no white spots. The voice too, though similar, is not identical. Both species have been seen around Szczęśliwice, though the park isn't exactly an ideal spot for woodpeckers. How can it compare with Skaryszewski Park in Praga, with its hundred-year-old trees concealing tasty insects in the crevices of their cracked bark? That park is home to as many as five species of the woodpecker family. Perhaps the Syrians appreciated the damson trees, cherry trees and partly rotting poplars that are living out the rest of their lives here?

Last spring the Syrian woodpeckers vanished. They quite simply stopped hammering on dry branches and calling from the top of their favourite plum tree. Lesser spotted woodpeckers, which are about the size of starlings, appeared instead. For several days they diligently excavated a hole in the cut-off trunk of a willow. It must have been a real slog; you could say they had their beaks full. Then, when the hole was finally ready, a great spotted showed up and unceremoniously kicked out its little cousins. The lesser spotteds tried to scare it off, screeching as loud as they could, but the giant went to work at once. It widened the opening, deepened the hole, and a few days later its mate laid eggs in there.

Szczęśliwice has its own folklore, of course. It's the folklore of city outskirts that all of a sudden are promoted and begin to claim they belong to the city itself. In the park, traditionally called Glinki (The Clay Pits) by the locals, two cultures rub up against one another. The old anglers constitute the anarchistic element that disregards the ban on drinking alcohol in public places. They're talkative folk, and willingly share stories about the secret life of the ponds' deep reaches. In fact, every few years a body is fished out. Ten or fifteen years ago I regularly used to see daredevils jumping from a height into the dark, cloudy water. A good many human necks have been broken on the hard bottom. The clay pits, as Nowakowski wrote, were the site of various kinds of initiation.

The park has its legendary characters. For example the Chairman likes to sunbathe in summer, and never turns down a drink. He says hello to everyone. Likewise Roberto, whose skin by the middle of May is usually the colour of dark Silesian brick. Roberto likes to talk about birds. He once tipped me off about a kingfisher he'd spotted on the pond, and he noted correctly that thrushes find insects in the grass by listening with their head cocked to one side. Sitting still at the waterside has a meditative quality; the anglers and other regulars know a lot about the animals that live here and their habits.

Big-city culture is represented by the runners. This group, though, is not uniform. There are human robots with earbuds who make dozens of circuits of the park without getting out of breath. There are suffering runners who take too-long strides and sigh in relief when their phone announces in its artificial voice: 'Training complete.' And there are perfectly normal people: deep in thought, contented, sad. I don't think I've ever been alone in the park. There's always someone either jogging or fishing.

Waking up requires an effort, and so spring awakens only reluctantly. It opens one eye, then closes it again. The frosts let up for a while, but soon afterwards their icy grip returns. Puddles now thaw, now cover over with a thin coating of ice. Towards the end of February larks fly high overhead – I've heard their jarring calls. Starlings start chattering as early as the beginning of March. But the final signal for the end of winter is given by the gulls, which vanish in the middle of the month. Soon after that the woodpigeons return and the park fills at once with their hoarse cooing. They set to work immediately, weaving their crude, pancake-flat nests. Tits claim their territories, chiffchaffs count off with their loud calls. The Germans, a practical people, call it the way it sounds: *der Zilpzalp*. White cherry blossom appears at the start of April. Within a few days the petals lie scattered on the ground.

Spring means haste – and surprises. For who would have expected that here, in the middle of the city, on a little lake surrounded by housing estates, two nervous greylag geese would stop by out of the blue? That, stretching their necks out uneasily, they'd float here for a full hour? In April, amid the clayey dullness of last year's grass, bright, juicy new shoots are growing. The yellow forsythia will bloom soon, then after it the apple tree will blossom. In the middle of the month the park's first singer, the blackcap, will come back, though to begin with its song will be short and soft, as if it were warming up for a major performance. Soon the wood warbler will arrive – a small yellowish bird with a piercing voice that sounds like a coin rolling across a marble table-top.

It's a race. A race against time, and against the competition for the best nesting spot. No need to be fussy – a fence post, a gate handle, or the inside of a crumbling concrete street lamp will do. An elongated crevice in a large aspen. A short-toed treecreeper has sneaked in there – an unostentatious bird like a little brown mouse, with a long downcurved bill. If a Brit were walking with me today he'd probably be over the moon – the species is very rare in the Isles. May means helpless chicks calling their parents from tree branches, benches, lawns. And a mass of dead bodies, for nature is cruel to the weak and the defective, even in this pleasant family park. June smells obscenely of barberry.

I discovered it by chance. It was a sultry June evening; in the middle of a conversation I heard a strange voice coming from the reeds. At such a moment everything else gets relegated to second place. An unfamiliar call cannot be ignored. I tiptoed up to the reeds, but the bird sensed the movement. For a moment it fell silent, then it repeated its 'ow, ow', like a distant barking. To be on the safe side I recorded the sound, but I already had a suspect. It was a little bittern, a shy heron the size of a pigeon that wriggles its way lithely among reed stems. Light, nimble, in its ochre-coloured camouflage plumage it's almost invisible.

The next day I went back to the same place first thing in the morning. I leaned on the wooden quay fence and watched the line of reeds through my binoculars. I was in luck. After a moment a small bird with a long bill peeped out cautiously though, feeling that it was being observed, it quickly ducked back in. Now there was no doubt. It's easy to overlook such an inconspicuous form as it cuts across the surface of a lake. The little bittern flies low over the water. It flaps its wings a little like a raven. But it's given away by the bright, shiny patches on its wings. It sits, looks about quickly, and dives into the greenery. Or it stretches upwards, pretending it's one of the reeds swaying in the wind. From time to time I see it fall still at the water's edge in hopes of a passing fish. Immobile, focused entirely on its hunting, it looks as if someone had placed it there and then forgotten about it.

There are fewer and fewer of them – only 700 pairs in the whole of Poland. In the wild, their pondside nests are plundered by American mink, so they're moving ever more frequently into the towns. But the following spring the little bittern kept me waiting a very long time. I'd already given up hope, knowing how

The little bittern

many dangers await it on its way back from Africa. Changes of weather, predators and also hunters. Finally, on 16 May, from up on the slope I saw a movement in the reeds. It could have been a coot, or the great reed warbler that had been jabbering away here for the past few days. A moment of calm. Then one of the stalks visibly bent under the weight of some creature. Soon, very cautiously, a splendid cream-and-blue male climbed almost to the very tip of the reed, followed by the female in her camouflage colours. They rose lightly from their perch and flew soundlessly across to the opposite side of the pond.

I adore this park, though not in the summer. I've long outgrown the schoolchild's love of holidays. In the summer I have nothing to do here. In June, the birds virtually stop singing and they're hidden by foliage. The lawns turn into sun-scorched savannahs, and the greenery darkens with every day and loses its moist firmness. By the end of August, the dried leaves on the birches rustle like paper. The open-air swimming pool fills with an unbroken babble that drowns out even the noise of the traffic. Hundreds of people crowd together like penguins in a colony, contending fiercely for the smallest scrap of grass.

Stifling, lifeless, motionless air, and the torch of the sun from early morning. Starting from dawn, processions bearing inflatable crocodiles, loungers and towels with pictures of naked women. Hosts of shirtless men. A display of unappetising bodies and lopsided tattoos. Music from mobile phones. Ageing *homo sapiens* males wading in the water like overweight hippopotamuses. Half-dressed old ladies sunbathing. Avid guardians of heated grills; the smell of pee under every bush. And the rubbish. Heaps of cans, plastic packaging floating solemnly across the lake, and glass bottlenecks peeking coyly from the reeds.

It was around midnight when J. and I arrived. The location seemed at first glance unpromising. A snarl of train tracks, interspersed with islands of undergrowth, just outside Warsaw West Station. Neck-high grasses and thistles, less than two miles from the park. It was right here, amid the stink of heated railway sleepers, that a certain unremarkable-looking little bird had decided to stop off on its way north. A birder from Szczecin had been doing some work for Polish Rail in a nearby building. The job dragged on into the night; tired, he decided to take a break. He opened a window and in the stillness heard an unexpected sound.

'Teeroorooroo-twee-twee': Blythe's reed warbler was singing its habitual song. So even here, in this ugliest place in the world, something interesting can come along. Blythe's reed warbler is a particularly secretive bird that sings almost exclusively at night. For that reason it's more often heard than seen. By day, what's more, it's easily confused with one of its commoner relatives from the reed warbler family. How many Blythe's fly across Poland unnoticed each year? No one knows. In any case, for this lover of rocky scenery we had to scramble a good way along the embankment. From far off, the Palace of Culture gazed at us through the white eye of its clock. Trains were rattling by inches away; then, when the rumble of the wheels slowly faded, from a dark mass of bushes came: 'teeroorooroo-twee-twee'.

The first (and so far only) record of a Blythe's nesting in Poland is from 2011 in Podlasie in the north-east, where it likes to stop during its migration. I go up to the bush, shine my torch on it and, though the bird is probably only a few metres from me, all I can see are leaves and their uncanny shadows. The warbler does not stop singing. Suddenly a small dark shape flits from one branch to another. A moment later the song comes from a different bush. Blythe's reed warbler likes best of all to live in flooded meadows with stands of willows, from the Baltics all the way to Siberia. It evidently took a liking to Podlasie. Actually, more and more species from the East are appearing regularly in Poland. It's said that they're expanding, but I think we're okay with that kind of expansion.

Right by the Blythe's, two other birds are transmitting ceaselessly. They are its close relations, marsh warblers, perhaps the most ecstatic avian imitators known to science. They're capable of singing their crazy improvisations for hours on end, looping their melodies around, abruptly changing tempo and rhythm. According to Françoise Dowsett-Lemaire, who's conducted research on the subject, marsh warblers have no song of their own whatsoever. Their singing is a brilliant mash-up of sounds they've overheard. As David Rothenberg writes in his book *Why Birds Sing*, the marsh warbler is simply a masterful DJ. I listen to the mad medley. I hear: barn swallow; some unidentified whistlings; greenfinch; mysterious crackles; and something that sounds like a MIDI synthesizer. The unfamiliar sounds are probably voices that the young birds heard during their first winter in East Africa. Singing is all very well, but it seems the females select their mate based on the amount of territory they occupy. So what's it about? Why do birds sing at all?

There are of course many reasons. Above all, males attract a partner with their song, and inform the competition about the territory they occupy. Throughout the year voices can be heard announcing: 'I'm here.' There's also the universal language of warning. The screech of an alarmed jay is understood by all the animals in the woods. Birds, Rothenberg writes, have always sung well; we're the ones whose tastes are forever changing. In 1717 came publication of *The Bird Fancyer's Delight*, a collection of works that people were to play to their canaries and budgerigars. The idea was to 'teach them to sing', to convince them to replace their whistles and chirps with conventional tunes. But today, Rothenberg points out, what once seemed jarring now sounds different to ears accustomed to free jazz, the twelve-note scale, and scratching.

In the 1920s British cellist Beatrice Harrison moved to the country and began practising outdoors in the evening. She heard the local nightingales diffidently joining in during her music-making. After a while they would enter on a full-voiced song whenever she started to play. In 1924, after much persuasion, she convinced Lord Reith, the then director general of the BBC, to broadcast the first music concert recorded in the open air. The crew set up a microphone in front of the bush, while Harrison, dressed in an evening gown, began to play. Whether it was because the birds had stage fright, or they didn't like the programme, or perhaps the technicians scared them away – in any case, the cello played alone for a good hour. It looked like being a flop.

Fifteen minutes before the end of the broadcast a nightingale added its voice to Dvořák's *Songs My Mother Taught Me*. In telling this story, Rothenberg permits himself a touch of scepticism. Was what the listeners experienced not 'naive anthropomorphism, or a desire to hear music where there was simply sound?' Perhaps the nightingale had merely been trying to drown out the instrument? Be that as it may, the broadcast was a huge success; Harrison received 50,000 letters of congratulation (!). The cello and nightingale concert was repeated live every year for twelve years. Later the avian singer performed solo, until 1942, when the rumble of approaching bomber squadrons crept into the background. The producer, not wishing to sow panic, cut short the broadcast.

There's no point in repeating all of Rothenberg's marvellous book. I'll summarise just one other charming story featuring the musical genius Wolfgang Amadeus Mozart. According to his expense book, on 27 May 1784 the composer purchased a starling – but not because he was especially fond of birds. This starling sang his Piano Concerto in G major, finished on 12 April that year! How could it have happened since the work had not yet been performed? Coincidence can almost certainly be ruled out. Mozart, who was in the habit of whistling in public, may have slipped the starling the tune. Yet the bird allowed himself a minor adjustment: he changed G to G sharp. In Rothenberg's view, the arrangement was ahead of its time.

Autumn means the colour of leaves maturing in the sun; in October they rustle underfoot in the multi-coloured avenues of trees. Warm light. Cool mornings. Dusk falling quickly. Disorientated ducks, scared away from suburban waters by hunters, land on the clay-pit pond. Tufted ducks look around warily with their yellow eye, but still they sometimes spend a few hours here. They never climb out onto the bank. But not because they feel uneasy in the city. Tufted ducks belong to the family of diving ducks, and they're unable to waddle around after park visitors the way mallards do. They can seek food down to a depth of ten metres, but on land their bellies rub awkwardly against the ground.

In September the time of transit well and truly begins, and the busy city below seems to make no impression on the travelling birds. By night geese can clearly be heard calling to one another. In the early morning a key of cranes passes high overhead, but the street noise swallows up their loud clangour. Around midday black cross-shaped buzzards circle. And when the daylight fades, the reeds come alive with a chorus of cheeps and chirps. During the day the starlings occupy fields around the city, but at night a countless throng of them descends upon the park. The immense flock leaves an unrepeatable expression of surprise and unease on the faces of passers-by. There are more and more birds, as if they were conferring before some vital decision. An hour before dusk the flock begins its spectacle.

Sometimes over the neighbourhood car park, sometimes above the reed-encircled clay pit, several groups, each comprising hundreds of birds, rise into the sky. The spherical masses mingle together in flight and, suddenly changing direction, they take on unexpected shapes. Then they gather together again, so compact that they become a single dark body. When they pass close by, the hum of thousands of wings, the whistle of millions of feathers, is plainly audible. A moment later they spread out into a long dark tongue, then all at once break into the atoms of individual birds. This huge morphing, openwork creature runs riot all the way till nightfall. The synchronisation and precision of its movements are astounding – it's as if the flock were governed by a single collective mind. The show is repeated several evenings in a row.

In late autumn, before the mirror of the water is coated with crystalline ice, a Canada goose appears. It's cautious, and swims away augustly whenever a dog appears on the horizon. It looks somehow alien – a large solitary goose amid ducks and coots. As its name suggests, it has its roots on another continent. It was introduced to British parks for decoration. A large, impressive bird with black neck and white cheeks, floating majestically upon a lake, it went well with white swans. The problem was that the Canada geese soon got bored of floating. They turned feral and began colonising new territory.

What was to be done with them? An ecosystem is a precise mechanism. Every creature has its place in it and its assigned task. There isn't exactly such a thing as a vacant slot. An aggressive newcomer can be a threat to insufficiently assertive autochthons – especially those that eat the same diet and inhabit a similar environment. That's how it was, for instance, with sparrows that were released by bird lovers. It was thanks to human beings that that little home-loving bird conquered almost the entire world. In its new location it put its powerful beak to good use and drove away the less robust competition. Starlings, by the way, acted just as uncouthly too.

A short blonde woman with a miniature bulldog tells me that the Canada goose had been introduced by a local developer so a neighbourhood pond would look nice. But the bird got bored of its surroundings and was fed only irregularly, so in the end it ran out of patience and moved to our little lake. Here the large goose is a sensation. People reach for their mobile phones when they see it. Frowning in concentration, they choose their framing and zoom in on their touch screen. Will they show any interest later in the bird that crossed their path? Will they ever go looking for that photograph of the goose amid their thousands of pictures of breakfasts, children, holidays?

THE FALCON MAN

'The first bird I searched for was the nightjar, which used to
nest in the valley.'

A round, bespectacled face, lost in thought, gazes from the
photograph. Thick lenses, receding hair, chin resting on a hand.
An ageing, melancholy man. He looks a little like a koala bear.
Until recently we knew very little about John Alec Baker. It
wasn't even clear what his middle name was – he used only his
initials. Quiet and modest, he lived unnoticed. The bio note on
the cover of his first book states that he and his wife live in Essex,
he doesn't have a telephone and doesn't like social occasions. He
left school at seventeen, then worked felling trees and pushing
a book cart at the British Museum, among other jobs. He was
forty-one when his first book came out: *The Peregrine*.

It's only recently that a few new facts have emerged to fill out
Baker's rather tame biography. He attended the renowned King
Edward VI Grammar School in his home town of Chelmsford.
His schoolmates recalled that despite his feeble eyesight he was
a pretty good cricketer. He was always in poor health; since
childhood he suffered from rheumatism, and often missed

school. He read a lot. Geology, Pablo Neruda, history of opera, Ted Hughes. For most of his life he worked at the Automobile Association, though he didn't even have a driving licence. He would sometimes get a lift from his wife, Doreen, who was nine years younger than him. He fell in love with birds relatively late in life, but it was a passionate love.

He got around on foot or by bicycle. It took Baker ten years to gather the material for his first book. In it, he collapsed that decade into six months. It's a bird journal kept from October to April. Continually dissatisfied with the result, he rewrote it in its entirety five times before he submitted the manuscript to a publisher. *The Peregrine* was recognised as a literary masterpiece, and its author received the respected Duff Cooper Prize. I'm awed by the richness of this book, the dazzling way in which Baker crosses the boundaries of linguistic conventions for nature writing. Of language in general. Nouns that turn into verbs. Verbs that flutter out of adjectives. The deep, careful rhythm of every phrase. The sentences could be broken up into lines and the prose turned into a long poem.

In 2005, *The Peregrine* was reissued in the New York Review Books Classics series. In his introduction, Robert Macfarlane calls the work 'an undeniable masterpiece'. I'm despondent to think how many things in it I do not understand. 'I swooped through leicestershires of swift green light.' I'm unable to translate that sentence into Polish, and I feel, rather than know, that it is beautiful. It sounds like music. I adore the boldness of the metaphors, the unconstrained synaesthesia. For Baker makes us smell sounds, look at scents. We have to grasp the impressions of one sense by way of another. His imagination knows no boundaries. I didn't know it was possible to write about nature in such a way.

Chelmsford is only half an hour by train from London, and it's neither a run-down suburb nor a resentful mass of tower blocks. It's not a dormitory town, though the place is a little sleepy. Its residents seem to appreciate the calm, and the closeness of the capital is not a source of frustration. They don't appear to be bothered by the fact that Chelmsford's only claim to fame is having the smallest cathedral in England. Everything here is on a human scale, as it were. At a kiosk run by a gentleman in a turban, in the small magazine section I find two birding publications. In colour, on good quality paper, produced like lifestyle monthlies. Delightful.

A small flock of waxwings chatter in the elms in front of St John's Church. It's been overcast since morning, but Finchley Avenue turns out to be a sunlit street of bright, detached houses. Baker was brought up at number 28. A young woman comes to the door. I see hesitation in her eyes, for the situation is a bit strange. Two people from Poland are asking about a writer who once lived in her house. The conversation takes place on the doorstep: she doesn't know anything, she's never heard of him. A pigeon rises from the roof in a clatter of wings. The windows on the other side of the house look out over a park. It's so peaceful here that when, half an hour later, we go back to the corner of Elm Road and Moulsham Street, the same greenfinch is still singing from the top of a tree. Or maybe it's its double? How would Baker have conveyed this voice? A chattering, pulsating song devoid of any melody. A sound that's easy to overlook in the confusion of springtime voices. I envy Baker. For myself, I'm unable to go beyond commonplaces and the most obvious associations. Or take the nightjar: when I bring to mind its monotonous song, I can think only of being inside an MRI scanner, whereas Baker's description is sheer poetry.

'Its song is like the sound of a stream of wine spilling from a height into a deep and booming cask. It is an odorous sound, with a bouquet that rises to the quiet sky. In the glare of day it would seem thinner and drier, but dusk mellows it and gives it vintage.'

It's hard to question the artful beauty of the language, but Baker has been accused of invention. No one witnessed the writer's sightings. It's been suggested that what he saw were reared birds, not wild peregrines wintering in Essex. There were very few such birds by the sixties, and in a country so crazy about birdwatching someone else would have noticed them. The suspicion arose that Baker mistook kestrels, smaller and very common in the English provinces, for peregrine falcons. Peregrines hovering over their prey or walking across a field and catching insects thrown up by the plough? No one had seen such a thing before. And why were there so many dead bodies of birds hunted by the peregrine? Over 600 of them have been counted in Baker's book. Anyone who's spent time in the field knows that you don't often see victims being torn apart. Does this diminish the value of the book? Scientifically, perhaps, but *The Peregrine* is after all a testimony to a literary obsession.

'The 'pee-wit' calls of plover grew louder as the sun declined. Standing among oaks and birches, I saw between the trees the dark curve of a peregrine scything smoothly up the green slope of the valley. Fieldfares fled towards the trees. Some thudded down into bracken, like falling acorns.'

After the success of *The Peregrine*, J. A. Baker settled on Marlborough Road with his wife and lived out his days. We knock. The door is opened by Bryan Clark, a cheerful fellow in a scarf and padded house slippers. He's a character. A journalist specialising in the mining industry. He uses words in such a way that I don't always follow what he means. He can't invite us in, he's busy, but he tells us about a Mr Biskupek, a Pole, who married his cousin. And he explains that the Clarks come from the same clan as the family of former Prime Minister David Cameron. For some time now a thick snow has been falling.

But Mr Clark unhurriedly finishes his story and declares phlegmatically: 'Am I mistaken, or has it started to snow?' He never met Baker, but heard from friends that he was shy, a bit of a loner.

We go to talk to the neighbours, Mr and Mrs Butler, who lived next door to the Bakers for twenty years. They sit us down on their sofa. I'm given coffee in an Arsenal mug. What was Baker like? 'Straaange,' Mrs Butler says, raising her eyebrows meaningfully. He loved only birds. He and his wife Doreen were ill-matched – she sang in a choir, liked company, while he was closed off, withdrawn. Though Mr Butler remembers how Baker once saw a man shooting at birds with an airgun in the old cemetery behind the house. That crank and introvert, with his arthritis that caused terrible back pain, flew into such a rage that he leapt the fence in a single bound and gave chase. The terrified shooter fled.

The cemetery lies right behind the houses of the Butlers and Mr Clark. Most of the tombstones are in the Gothic style from the turn of the previous century. Here lies Alfred Darby, estate agent, and the modest Ruth, no more than 'sister of the above'. Pigeon feathers – scraps from the feast of some bird of prey – and an overwrought robin that's virtually choking on its own song. I take two steps forward and it falls silent, ducks down, and watches me tensely, but right away it resumes its singing. I'm so close I could reach out and snatch it up, but the robin couldn't care less. I'm not a robin, I don't count. Now it's focused exclusively on finding a mate and defending its territory. It's serious work. Robins may look sweet, but they're capable of fighting to the death over their own piece of the garden. On the internet there are endless questions about what to do when such a bird keeps obsessively attacking its own reflection in the window of a parked car.

'For a bird, there are only two sorts of bird: their own sort, and those that are dangerous. No others exist. The rest are just harmless objects, like stones, or trees, or men when they are dead.'

Baker meditates. In his notes there's a calming order, a rhythm that returns like a mantra. Waking up. The peregrine flies to the nearest stream, bathes, dries, preens. It dozes. Then it rises and circles, gathers speed, plays, frightens other birds with mock attacks. It hunts and then eats its prey. It rests. Patrols the area. Looks for a place to spend the night. Falls asleep. At times there's even less afoot. Baker finds the remains of a gutted pigeon. The remnants of a gull. Fresh and still warm, or old, dry and stiff. Nothing is going on. Marc Cocker writes in the introduction that Baker is 'a master of emptiness and stagnation'. His writing is the opposite of television imagery, which focuses exclusively on action. It's a song of praise to stillness and patience. 'Nothing happens,' Baker is capable of writing.

A peregrine falcon

On the small Chelmer River, similar to the Świder near Warsaw, an early spring is beginning. The stalks of last year's weeds shine white in the bright, still wintry sun. Every other moment a short, violent rain falls, and leaden clouds drift overhead. Wind and a rainbow. Rabbits squat in the grass near the gates of the houses. Only at the last minute do they rise and hop sluggishly away. Moorhens, so secretive and timid in Poland, paddle at the water's edge. The cold wind goes right through you; I'm glad I don't have rheumatism. Fields begin right outside the town. Lapwings chase one another in their jerky flight; a flock of thrushes bounces about on a pasture. I look closely: fieldfares, redwings, song thrushes. Great Britain lies on the ocean, and every year American species blown off course by some storm are spotted here.

In the riverside bushes a white cotton ball with a long tail is flitting about. It's a long-tailed tit of the British *rosaceus* subspecies, whose head is darker than the Polish kind. I look up into the sky in hopes that one of Baker's peregrines will fly by, but the only bird of prey is a kestrel bobbing on the wind like a child's kite. A splendid male with a light blue head, looking for pickings in the previous year's grasses. It hangs there for a moment, its wings flapping rapidly, then plummets to earth. A white wagtail is strutting about in the mud – in fact a pied wagtail, the *yarrelli* subspecies, another local speciality, which has a black back, not grey as in Poland. Emerald-green streaks of kingfishers zoom after one another in the springtime drabness. A grey wagtail is pattering across the rocks by the lock – despite its Polish name of 'mountain wagtail', it's found in the valleys too. It constantly flicks its amazingly long tail, which it uses like a tightrope walker to keep its balance. I reach the first lock, the midpoint on a route that Baker often took.

The landscape of Essex, flat and treeless, for Baker is a mysterious, almost mythical realm. The south wood, the north wood, the ford. Certain places can be identified. A 200-foot high chimney, or a wooden spire that a wren climbs up. An anonymous land without familiar place names. The banal scenery of the English countryside, that has been described hundreds of times, for him seems almost exotic. Baker doesn't say a word about humans; he shuns them as do the peregrines to which he devotes all his attention. He strives for the birds' acceptance, wants to please them. He always wears the same clothing, moves cautiously because falcons are afraid of what is unpredictable. He admires the dark sickle of their silhouette, and revels in the spectacle of death, the myriad birds that take flight in consternation. Every day he goes one step closer; he's unable to help himself. He won't and he can't.

After the success of *The Peregrine*, Baker gave up his job and wrote *The Hill of Summer*, a poetic story of an English spring. His rheumatism got worse and with it his misanthropy. The ever-stronger medications induced a tumour. Baker was no longer able to walk. Entirely dependent on his wife, he became insufferable. He refused to let her have guests, demanded that their relatives announce their visits in advance. Doreen put up with him to the end. He died on 26 December 1987; he was cremated, and his ashes were buried in Chelmsford. Soon afterwards his wife moved to another town nearby.

I walk around the cemetery in dazzling sunlight, but I can't find his grave. Somewhere among the trees a green woodpecker is laughing at me maliciously.

FRANÇOIS MITTERRAND'S
LAST SUPPER

HER NAME WAS MARTHA AND she was twenty-nine years old at the time of her death. She passed away at the Cincinnati Zoo on 1 November 1914. She was the last representative of her species, the last passenger pigeon. She never had any offspring. Only a hundred years earlier, the passenger pigeon was perhaps the most populous species on earth. In the early nineteenth century Alexander Wilson, the father of American ornithology, claimed to have observed a flock of over 2 billion birds. In 1871 there were over 100 million of them nesting in the woods near Sparta, Wisconsin. The disappearance of the passenger pigeon is one of the most moving examples of the destruction wrought by human activity.

'Imagine a thousand threshing machines operating at full throttle, steamship whistles blaring, and freight trains thundering across bridges: combine all this commotion into one and you will be able to imagine the terrifying sound' – thus wrote a journalist from the *Fond du Lac Commonwealth Reporter*, describing the sound of the wings of millions of pigeons. Trees came crashing down under the weight of the birds sitting in them. The sight was so terrifying that hunters dropped their guns out of fear. Though not of course all of them. Passenger pigeons ruined the crops, and so they were slaughtered unrelentingly. They were peppered with birdshot, knocked down with sticks, their roosts were burned.

The last wild passenger pigeon died in 1900 at the hands of a boy with an air rifle. The bird was stuffed, with buttons in place of eyes. And that was what they called it: Buttons. It turned out that the huge flocks could defend themselves perfectly well against 'conventional' predators, but not against humans. When the population reached a critical point the birds quite simply ceased to reproduce. In the same year of 1900 Republican congressman John F. Lacey of Iowa introduced into Congress a bill proposing the first legislation aimed at protecting nature; this became known subsequently as the Lacey Act. Referring to the passenger pigeon, he stormed: 'We have offered a repulsive display of massacre and devastation that ought to serve as a warning to mankind.'

The European roller is a bird of stunning, almost disconcerting beauty. The sapphire blue of its wings glinting in summer sunlight offers a curious contrast to the muted palette of our meadows and woods. Despite intensive conservation efforts, the prognosis is not good. Over the past thirty years the roller population of Poland has gone from 1,000 pairs to thirty-five. In the west of the country the species died out long ago; the one remaining stronghold is the Kurpie Plain in the north-east. There are also one or two pairs living in the Podkarpackie region in the south, but that's an isolated community likely to disappear in the coming years.

The question is whether there is any hope at all for the Polish rollers, or whether the gene pool is already too small for the species to survive. As early as 1972, Jan Sokołowski wrote in his *Birds of Poland*: 'In the Poznań region, in Pomerania and in Silesia it occurs only in extensive forests, and never in great numbers... To the east of the Vistula, by contrast, it is common and, when travelling by train, by the time we are approaching Warsaw we may see rollers perched on telegraph wires.' In a guide to the capital published in the 1980s I read that rollers could be observed in the suburb of Powsin. Today you have to drive for miles around the Kurpie region, which after all is not so large, to spot the characteristic outline of the turquoise-coloured bird lying in wait for its prey.

During migration, thousands of rollers perish in the countries of the Mediterranean Basin. And not just rollers. Hunters do not single out any particular species. Millions of birds die, rollers among them. It's a sobering thought that, while we spend considerable sums on the protection of this precious sapphire-blue creature, our entire microscopic population can be wiped out by a single person. And not necessarily a hungry person. Many people shoot primarily for sport or to show off on social media. Every year thousands of photographs of killed birds find their way onto the internet. And though such killings are illegal almost everywhere, in the troubled countries of the Middle East combating poaching is not a high priority.

A few years ago the American edition of *National Geographic* magazine featured an article by Jonathan Franzen titled 'Last Song'. The writer describes the slaughter of birds during their migration across the Mediterranean region. He does his best to be objective, weighing the arguments and reconciling his sensitivities as a well-fed Westerner with the interests of people for whom hunting is the only source of livelihood. A bird seller at an Egyptian market, seeing the disapproval in Franzen's face, says: 'You Americans feel bad about the birds, but you don't feel bad about dropping bombs on someone's homeland.' There's a painful truth in those words, though it would be easy enough to snap back that sensitivity to natural beauty doesn't exclude sensitivity to human suffering. But Franzen doesn't respond.

The essence of the conflict is clearly depicted in a scene that Franzen describes. An acacia grove in the middle of the desert. An oasis in a sea of sand. A group of Bedouin teenagers from well-to-do homes are killing time by killing birds that are resting among the trees. In front of a tent a yellow wagtail is hopping about, 'a tiny, confiding, warm-blooded, beautifully plumaged animal that had just flown several hundred miles across the desert,' writes Franzen. But the young hunter is neither charmed by the beauty of the bird nor moved by its vulnerability. He shoots his air rifle at it without a second thought. He misses. The wagtail flies off. For the Bedouin it's 'the fish that got away'. For the writer it is 'a rare moment of relief'.

Westerners often anthropomorphise birds. They endow them with character, ascribe human virtues to them. For these Egyptians they're simply animals, no one makes a fuss over them. Killing a bird is no different from killing a fish. And that's how it's always been in some places. The problem, though, is that hunting methods have changed. A hunter armed with a club is considerably less effective than one carrying a rifle with a precision sight. These days it's common to lure birds with MP3 recordings. Nets of fine nylon thread cover almost the entire coastline during the migration season. According to Franzen, the nets catch up to 100,000 quail exhausted by their flight across the sea. The Egyptians Franzen speaks to explain that they don't kill local species, only 'foreign' migratory birds.

(In February 2014 Albania introduced a two-year moratorium on hunting. Both birds and mammals were protected. The decision was said to have been inspired by Franzen's text.)

The great auk. This large bird, over eighty centimetres tall, once lived in the northern seas from Canada to Norway. The great auk spent most of its life in the water, only reluctantly and awkwardly climbing out onto the rocky coast. Its upright figure was reminiscent of the penguin. It laid a single egg, raised its chick, then returned to the sea. It had small vestigial wings incapable of supporting it in flight. There was nothing odd about this – the wings served as oars, and the great auk was an unparalleled swimmer and diver.

Auks were hunted as far back as the Palaeolithic era. Ornaments fashioned from their beaks have been found in the graves of fishermen and sailors from that time. Later accounts by mariners speak of rocky islands so densely populated by the birds that it was impossible to make your way among them. Great auks were mercilessly destroyed for their meat and their feathers. On the barren islands of the far north their oily, waterproof plumage and plump bodies also served sailors as fuel. It was for that reason that the largest colony, on the island of Funk, was wiped out (when Europeans first landed there it's estimated that the population consisted of 100,000 pairs). Another colony on the coast of Iceland, surrounded by cliffs and inaccessible to humans, was obliterated by a volcanic eruption. Towards the end of the eighteenth century it was becoming clear that the great auk's situation was critical. Museums wished to have a specimen of the disappearing bird. Rich snobs wanted the eggs of the elusive great auk to add to their collections.

This ghastly contest came to an end on 3 July 1844, when three Icelandic fishermen landed on the island of Eldey. They spotted a pair of birds; the female had managed to lay an egg on the cliffs. The auks fled, leaving their treasured offspring behind, but their bodies, so nimble in the water, moved too slowly on land. Jón Brandsson and Sigurður Ísleifsson killed both adult birds, while Ketill Ketilsson went down in history as the chump who smashed the single remaining egg. The auks were sold for the equivalent of £9. The eggshell was tossed away as being of no value.

The civilisation of Ancient Egypt depended on the annual caprices of the Nile – the flooding river carried fertile silt into the cultivated fields. Drought meant hunger. But the river offered various kinds of sustenance. In the thickets of papyrus sedge along the riverbanks, migrating birds were hunted. From wall paintings we know that for this purpose weapons resembling present-day boomerangs were used – curved pieces of wood with a sharpened edge. A relief from the tomb of Mereruka (twenty-third century BCE) depicts the hunting of quail and other birds hiding in the grain. Commonly used were large nets in a wooden frame that were thrown onto a feeding flock. At times so many birds were caught that not all of them could be eaten. Greylag geese, tamed and kept by households, were the ancestors of present-day domestic geese.

A painting from the tomb of Prince Nefermaat shows three pairs of birds of different species: red-breasted geese, greater white-fronted geese, and taiga bean geese. It's clear that the artist had closely studied their bodily proportions and details of their plumage. For many years the image was dated to 2600 BCE; it's only recently that suspicions have been raised that this masterpiece, known as the Egyptian *Mona Lisa*, is a fake. Independently of whether the author is an ancient artist or the discoverer of the image, the nineteenth-century painter Luigi Vassalli, geese did in fact occupy an important position in Egyptian religion. They were a symbol of Geb, a second-rank god who played a first-rank role. It was from eggs laid by him that the sun was born. He was the progenitor of other 'bird gods': Isis (sometimes depicted as a kite) and her son

Horus – the man with the head of a falcon, lord of the universe, sometimes identified with the current ruler, at other times accompanying him as a guardian. In one sculpted figure the falcon perches on the headrest of the throne and in a strangely human gesture protects with his wings the head of Khafre, a pharaoh who constructed one of the pyramids and also the Great Sphinx.

There was also Thoth, the ibis moon god, born from Horus's sperm, with his sickle-shaped bill. He it was who gave humans the alphabet. The African sacred ibis (in Polish it's called *ibis czczony*, or 'worshipped ibis') was venerated in Egypt. Herodotus maintained that killing such a bird meant the death penalty. Ibises were reared in temples dedicated to Thoth, and after death their bodies were embalmed. Archaeologists have discovered catacombs with the remains of millions of mummified ibises. When Egyptomania raged around the turn of the nineteenth and twentieth centuries, British historical artists would paint scenes of ibises being fed by priestesses in various states of undress.

❦

There's an expression, 'dead as a dodo'. It means finally and irrevocably gone. Human beings dealt swiftly with this large flightless pigeon native to Mauritius. They were certainly aided by the fact that the unfortunate dodo (*Raphus cucullatus*) was trusting and tame. Birds on isolated islands were not afraid of newcomers, being unaware of their destructive capabilities. People killed dodos for their meat, while their eggs and chicks were eaten by the pigs, rats and macaques brought by the Europeans. The last reliable report of a living bird comes from 1622. The most recent research indicates that the species died out in the 1690s. Flightless relatives of the dodo on neighbouring islands disappeared 100 years later.

No stuffed specimen has survived to the present day. We have only a skin-covered skull and a foot. In fact we don't even know for sure exactly what they looked like. For years the main source of information were drawings and paintings, the best known of which were by Roelandt Savery, from the 1620s. The artist had observed various exotic creatures in the menageries of the wealthy and included them in many of his paintings. He was especially fond of fantastical, harmonious landscapes depicting peaceful gatherings of animals. Predators among herbivores, lions, deer and ducks together. We can see the dodo for instance in *Landscape with Birds*, or in the lower right-hand corner of *Paradise*. The dodo was also painted by Roelandt's nephew Jan, though he probably copied from the work of his uncle.

It's currently believed that the Saverys' pictures are not an accurate portrayal of the dodo. The birds raised in captivity apparently had a tendency to eat excessively and were quite simply fat. Dodos in the wild were slimmer and are said to have been good runners. Scientists have at their disposal numerous dodo skeletons, to which flesh has been hypothetically added. An exhibit at the Natural History Museum in London shows one such reconstruction. A plaster form like those seen in Savery's paintings has been given grey feathers. Initially it was as plump as the birds in the pictures; it was made leaner only after an examination of the skeleton and an analysis of how much weight it was capable of bearing.

For a few years now I've been following the Facebook page of a Lebanese man called George. George regularly posts pictures of birds he has killed. Here's George with armfuls of song thrushes tied together by the head. He looks pleased with himself. He's wearing a camouflage jacket torn under one arm, and he's got a cigarette in his mouth. That's George – the manly look. Now here's George with a friend. Photogenically knitted brows, shotguns in hand, a tangled mass of small birds on the bonnets of their two jeeps. A few hundred of them, it looks like. Another picture shows a table strewn with dead birds, and in the corner the hand of a small child who's risen on tiptoe to take a look at the haul.

George devoted two whole photos to an injured cousin of the common buzzard known as the long-legged buzzard. The bird is perching on the ground with lowered wings. Blood can be seen on the paving stones; the picture was taken from close up. There's a furious mass of comments on the pictures, because George lets everyone have their say. He answers. He even wrote: 'Only God can judge me.' It's true that in this matter Lebanese law is exceptionally lacking. Regulations were proposed in 2004, introducing limits on numbers of birds from common species that can be hunted, and giving protection to, among other things, birds of prey, pelicans and storks. But they never came into force. An outdated law from 1995 is widely ignored. To give a sense of the scale of the problem, the Committee Against Bird Slaughter analysed pictures posted on social media alone. On 589 photographs they counted more than 13,000 killed birds belonging to 153 species. Among this number were endangered species: Egyptian vulture, lesser spotted eagle, night heron, European roller. The photographs came from only 400 web pages. It's estimated that there are 600,000 hunters in Lebanon (of whom only three per cent are registered).

I check out the pages of George's friends. This isn't some band of villagers killing for food (there aren't any people like that on Facebook); they're upper middle class. They're not afraid of being fined, they're well dressed, they have new cars, they travel the world. Jamil is an accountant. We can see pictures of his from Paris and Geneva; he has a good-looking wife and likes German shorthaired pointers. On his page he's proudly posted a photo of a dead nightjar. This nocturnal bird soundlessly gives chase to moths in the darkness. Of course it's illegal to hunt it, but shooting such an elusive bird is a cause for pride. Jamil is friends with Jad. The latter looks a little like Jason Statham and seems to know it. Square jaw, shaved head, stubbly beard and dark glasses. During the hunt he's hard-faced, but when he's photographed amid luxury his features soften and his face looks like a squashed doughnut. Like the others, at the weekend he turns into a ruthless killing machine.

Hunters from Lebanon, the better-off ones, like to travel. In late summer and autumn, for example, they go to Romania. Here they kill among other things turtle doves, quail and small songbirds. It's 'all inclusive'. The simplest analysis of the social media pages of the hunters shows clearly that official kill limits are frequently exceeded. The author of the article 'The Massacre of Europe's Songbirds' estimates that, of the 5 billion birds that fly to Africa and the Mediterranean region in the autumn, about 1 billion perish. Birds of prey are killed with poisoned carrion; loudspeakers playing recordings lure smaller birds into nets and glue traps. The birds land on branches covered with a thick paste that prevents them from taking flight again, and usually they die of exhaustion in the burning southern sun. In Malta, for instance, the murderous concoction is made from plums.

In the European Union there exists the so-called Birds Directive, which calls for the protection not just of the birds themselves but also of their habitat. Unfortunately member countries can create exceptions to these regulations. The killing of certain bird species eaten in French restaurants would land you in prison in Britain. A mistle thrush hunted in Romania has to be smuggled into Italy. The business is run by organised gangs; the birds are decapitated and partially dressed so as to make them difficult to identify. The scale of the operation is massive. Suffice it to say that in a single truck coming from Serbia the Italian border police found 130,000 birds packed tightly together.

In the Balkans and Romania it's mostly Italians who hunt. You can find them there at any time of year, in and out of season.

Italian hunters are permitted to take 100 skylarks per day out of Romania, but in reality they take many more. An organiser of hunting excursions boasted to the author of the article that the record holder shot 400 birds in one day. The company provided him with a folding chair so he wouldn't overtire himself. The chair was placed near a freshly mown field on which flocks of birds were feeding. The Romanian government is constantly easing restrictions that protect birds; in 2015, for example, they gave permission to shoot up to one third of the country's skylark population. Many hunters from Italy are CEOs of companies and banks, in a word potential investors, and the skylarks are bait.

On the subject of nature conservancy I've never read anything as powerful as Fred Bodsworth's *Last of the Curlews*. This book, first published in 1955, tells of the lastliving eskimo curlew, who is searching for a partner. It wanders alone, alone it defends a piece of tundra on which it seeks to build a shallow nest lined with leaves and grass. It drives away curlews of other species, and fiercely attacks a rough-legged buzzard patrolling the vicinity. Instinct tells it each year when to set off on its journey across two continents – from the Canadian far north to Patagonia.

The eskimo curlew was first described in 1772 by Johann Reinhold Forster. 'The locals call it wee-kee-me-nase-su; in the marshes it feeds on insects, grubs etc. It arrives in Fort Albany in April or early May; breeding takes place in the north; it returns in August and in great flocks continues south in the second half of September.' In 1861 Elliott Coues wrote that flocks being shot at by hunters would not fly away but only circle aimlessly overhead. One shot would kill up to twenty birds. The hunters called them dough-birds, because during the migration season they were so fat that the skin on their breasts burst when they hit the ground. Sometimes, when a sudden storm had pushed the curlews onto the open sea, they would land on the beach afterwards, too exhausted to take off again. Then humans would kill them with clubs.

By the beginning of the twentieth century ornithologists no longer had any doubts where all this was heading. 'Since 1892 only a small remnant of this once numerous species has visited the coast of Labrador [...]. It is clear that the eskimo curlew is vanishing – and is on a direct path to complete extinction,' wrote Charles W. Townsend and Glover M. Allen in an article published in 1907. Less than a decade later it was generally accepted that the species would not recover. The numbers of birds were so small that no one believed the population could be built back up. Ornithologists compared the massacre of the curlews to what had happened with the recently departed passenger pigeon.

Bodsworth's bird is a being like us – it has an inner life, it experiences sorrow and joy. It seeks happiness. It's easy to accuse the author of anthropomorphism, and that's a charge that often lands perceptive and valuable books in the children's literature section, along with stories about wise old owls and conceited crows. Humans resist the idea that animals feel. And that their feelings in some way resemble our own. What makes

Bodsworth's book so moving is precisely the attempt to see the world through the eyes of a bird. Driven by instinct, yet subject to emotions. It's not a naive perspective, though it's very remote from the way we usually look at animals.

After five years of waiting the curlew finally meets its mate. The courtship scenes are astounding. How does Bodsworth manage to make such a faithful description of the birds' behaviour simultaneously so touching? At times he simply makes the curlews human: 'They conversed endlessly in the darkness – the soft, lisping sounds rose lightly over the whistling of the wind beneath their wings, and the male was beginning to forget he had ever known the torment of solitude.' Perhaps it's unscientific, but in the end it's literature, engaged literature, aimed at educating fearless defenders of nature.

Alas – in order to rouse our anger and our opposition to human cruelty, the story cannot end well. The pair sit in a freshly ploughed field somewhere on the prairie. The other birds rise into flight when they see a tractor coming, but not the curlews. They trust to the strength of their wings, and linger till the last moment. Absorbed in the ecstasy of love, they pay no heed to the man who climbs down from the tractor. When the shots ring out, the curlews take to the air, but the female flies slower and slower. She gives a final cry and falls to earth. The male calls out to her, urges her to make an effort, but in vain. He spends the night next to her cold body, then flies north, led by his instinct, so as to go on stubbornly defending his territory as he waits for another female.

Bodsworth's book was turned into an hour-long animated

movie that came out in 1972. It was of course more popular than the book, though the cartoon *Last of the Curlews* is a merely a faithful adaptation. Stirring music, the scenes with the two birds huddling together, and the dramatic ending, all made a lasting impression on viewers. Not only children, though the film was above all aimed at them. Here the curlews were even more like human beings: 'They talked all night, planning their home in the north and their future family.'

The last pair of eskimo curlews were seen in 1962 in Galveston, Texas, by Sergeant Joseph M. Heiser Jr. They were feeding in the company of other birds, including several whimbrels, a species of curlew deceptively similar in appearance. Yet there was no mistaking them. The observers had eight telescopes between them and for almost an hour were able to check every diagnostic detail on the curlews wading through the grass. A year later, in Barbados another bird was shot (the body was identified by our old friend James Bond, who sent it to be displayed in the Natural History Museum in Philadelphia). Since that time, despite a handful of reports, there has been no confirmed sighting. At present the eskimo curlew is classified as 'critically endangered (probably extinct)'.

Birds are hunted in Poland too. Legally, during a specified season we can shoot at thirteen different species. The problem, though, is that the majority of hunters don't know the first thing about birds. After all, at first glance every duck in flight looks the same, especially in poor light. Many hunters don't even realise they're killing protected species. Why hunt birds at all? Just as in the case of deer, the argument is often the destruction of crops caused by, for example, large flocks of geese. Does hunting lead to a reduction in damage for farmers? Why does the list of game birds include for example the coot, which is never found on cultivated fields? What harm is caused by the forest-dwelling hazel grouse?

Opponents of bird-hunting often come up against the indomitable pathos of the term 'tradition'. When other arguments fail it is this 'tradition' that supposedly justifies shooting at ducks, geese, and coots. After all, our fathers and grandfathers did the same, so an attack on this practice becomes an attack on our identity, our history, our values. On Polishness. Yet to evoke those idyllic times when hunting was a fundamental part of everyday life is to ignore the fact that our world no longer resembles that earlier world in the slightest. In the present day hardly anyone eats wild birds; farm-raised poultry is so cheap that anyone can afford it. Shooting at birds is rather just a kind of thrilling sport.

The Milicz Ponds in the valley of the Barycz. Dug out in the thirteenth century by the ingenious Cistercians, to this day they're used for raising carp, and constitute a large nature reserve. Every year thousands of geese spend their nights safely on these extensive waters. Around eight in the morning the departure begins. The birds rise into the clear air. Geese are social creatures; the whole time they call out to one another, making sure they're flying with those they know, and their companions confirm that they're close by. The geese move to the neighbouring fields to feed on the corn stubble. It's not far, but the journey is a dangerous one. The edge of the pond constitutes the boundary of the reserve, and here hunters are already lying in wait to send their No. 2 ammunition into the flock. The cluster of lead shot expelled from a plastic cartridge usually hits several birds at once. If they don't perish on the spot, they die some time later from lead poisoning or infected wounds.

In France too there is a perpetual discussion about tradition – of the culinary kind. Famous chefs, prominent politicians, defenders of national identity, and the mass of refined gourmands cannot get over the fact that European regulations do not allow them to eat ortolan buntings. These are the small wild birds, relatives of the yellowhammer, that are said to have inspired the opening bars of Beethoven's Fifth Symphony. For many years now their numbers have been declining dramatically because, despite the ban, every year poachers trap almost 30,000 ortolans in the south of the country. The birds are then kept in darkened boxes and fattened up (the experience of night disorientates them and increases their appetite).

The sale, killing and eating of ortolans is of course forbidden but, in a country that prides itself on its cuisine, a blind eye is turned to law-breaking when such delicacies are at stake. The fattened birds, two or even three times their natural weight, end up in restaurants, where they are marinated in Armagnac so their innards become infused with alcohol. They are then placed in the oven. Ortolans are eaten whole (spitting out only the larger bones), a napkin being thrown over the diner's head to retain the splendid aromas. This pornographic example of cruelty (along with the way *foie gras* is produced, by the way) does not deter the true gourmet.

When François Mitterrand was dying of cancer, on his deathbed he ordered the following menu: thirty Marennes oysters, *foie gras*, a capon, and, as the pièce de résistance, two ortolans. Accompanied by a sweet Sauternes. Even the French acknowledged that there was something unseemly in this festival of gluttony. The taste of ortolan also delighted Jeremy Clarkson, a motoring journalist and celebrity known for speaking his mind. In the British TV programme *Jeremy Clarkson Meets the Neighbours* he was given a plate with a small roast bird, which he ate with relish. He explained that he had not paid for the ortolan and so everything was in accordance with the law. The BBC received thousands of complaints. Many of his fans, even those convinced that this boorish presenter was the last honest voice in an insincere world of political correctness, felt that this time he'd gone too far.

⟜⟜

Birds don't die from guns alone. The majority are victims of civilisation more broadly conceived. In the United States hunters kill 15 million birds a year. It's a sizeable number, but figures provided by the American Bird Conservancy reveal that it's only the tip of the iceberg. It turns out that the greatest

An ortolan bunting mid-song

human-related danger to birds comes from domestic cats. Every year these animals, roaming free outdoors, kill one-and-a-half to three-and-a-half billion birds in the United States! That means that every American cat has dozens of dead birds on its conscience. And counter-measures are very simple. The most effective, of course, is to keep the cat indoors. But even putting a collar with a small bell around its neck will save the lives of 50 per cent of the birds.

According to researchers at the University of Exeter, in the years 1980–2009 the bird population of Europe decreased by 421 million. The research covered twenty-five countries. The decline affects above all the commonest species such as sparrows, starlings and skylarks, a fact that points to the dramatic degradation of the environment. That figure of 421 million is even more striking when we realise it's 20 per cent of the entire bird population of Europe.

Worst off of all are birds that inhabit farmland, who perish because of intensified farming methods and the widespread use of chemicals. We cut through habitats with our network of roads. We force birds into terrain for which we ourselves have not yet found a use. We are egotistical and shortsighted. I found a sad symbol of these policies in the Biebrza Valley in Spring 2015. The central basin of the river is a veritable nature sanctuary where the rarest Polish birds can be found. From April, on the meadows here the few remaining black grouse (which twenty years ago were still classified as game birds) can be heard making their cackling call; in May, the sedge marshes resound with the clicking sounds of the great snipe. It's six in the morning, the sunshine is blinding, and

I'm looking at an alder swamp where one of the few pairs of Polish greater spotted eagles have their home. A few miles beyond the wood (no distance at all for a bird in flight) the silver blades of a wind farm glint in the sun.

CREDITS